PRAISE FOR
FROM DEBATE TO DIALOGUE: Using the Understanding Process to Transform Our Conversations

Bronze Winner of 1999 Colorado Independent Publishers Award

"I enjoyed reading this book very much. It has new perspectives I had not heard of before. A very timely and cogent book for today's world!"

Judge, Colorado Independent Publishers Association Book Awards

"*From Debate to Dialogue* is simple to read and profound in its impact. The book defines both a behavior and a way of thinking that makes a positive difference in the bedroom and the boardroom. I am recommending it to all my clients and friends."

Judith Cannon, Consultant
Dallas, Texas

"Now Flick has created a bridge between debate and dialogue that is practical and applicable in every day communication."

Carol Massanari, Ph.D.
University of Kentucky

"Using Flick's *Understanding Process* can propel participants' understanding and appreciation for the impact of differences on their lives and the lives of others at a level that assures healing and supports growth."

Carolyna Smiley-Marquez, Ph.D.
Founder, Diversity Associates International

"Excellent examples! Flick's communication concepts really spring to life."

Diane R. Koslow, Ph.D.
Clinical Psychologist
Washington, D.C.

"*From Debate to Dialogue* is a valuable tool in enhancing the resolution of conflict process."

James Norman, Ph.D.
SSJ Consultants
Ottawa, Ontario

"This book provides useful tools and perspectives that will help our organization build greater inclusiveness among staff, students and Board of Trustees."

Joan Welsh, President
Hurricane Island Outward Bound School
Rockland, Maine

FROM DEBATE
TO
DIALOGUE

Using the
Understanding
Process
to Transform
Our
Conversations

Deborah L. Flick, Ph.D.

ORCHID
PUBLICATIONS

Boulder, Colorado

PRINTING HISTORY
First printing: August, 1998
Second printing: September, 1999
Third printing: September, 2000
Fourth printing: August, 2002

ISBN: 0-9663671-0-3

Published by Orchid Publications
P.O. Box 895
Boulder, CO 80306-0895
(303) 443-5677

Cover Design: Mike Jenson, Jenson Advertising

CONTENTS

PART I
GETTING ACQUAINTED WITH THE UNDERSTANDING PROCESS

PART II
APPLICATIONS: TRANSFORMING OUR CONVERSATIONS

PART III
GOING FORWARD

ACKNOWLEDGMENTS

The *Understanding Process* has been a work in progress for many years. During this time many people including clients, workshop participants, family, friends and colleagues have generously contributed their ideas, insights and encouragement. Many more people have supported the development of the *Understanding Process* and the writing of this book than can be mentioned in this space.
Specifically, I want to thank
Marty Marquez, Pamela Bliss, Benson Walker, Christine Testolini, Kirstin Marr, Keith Langeneckert, Mary Scheidler, John Dawson, and Sue Phillips, and especially Ira Becker, my lifepartner, who has supported and encouraged me at every step.

PART I

GETTING ACQUAINTED WITH THE UNDERSTANDING PROCESS

In Search of an Antidote to the Debate Culture

Increased understanding will naturally lead to mutual respect.
Fourteenth Dalai Lama

- How can we express different points of view without becoming polarized?

- How can we replace destructive stereotyping of each other with understanding and concern?

- How do we listen so that positive change can occur?

- How can we create innovative, inspired solutions?

- How can we create and maintain organizations that are productive, flexible and easily adapt to constant change?

Providing a direct method called the *Understanding Process* for entering into dialogue about any issue, especially difficult or controversial ones, is the primary purpose of this book. This alternative to *Conventional Discussion* or debate transforms our conversations in real and meaningful ways and fosters effective, lasting change. Throughout the book we will explore how using the Understanding Process enhances results in a variety of contexts including: leadership, teamwork, public meetings, interpersonal conflicts, and valuing diversity.

Conventional Discussion Differs From Dialogue

The word "discuss" originally stems from Latin and means "to dash to pieces; to scatter apart; to quash or crush." Dispute, debate, heated argument, and wrangle are common synonyms.[1] "Conventional" refers to a mode of conduct widely accepted by society. Thus, the term "Conventional Discussion" characterizes a common style of interaction in which we "dash to pieces" others ideas and opinions (if not the person themselves). We often do this in the name of being right or "getting to the truth of the matter." In this regard James Thurber observed, "Discussion in America means dissent."

Many of us are more familiar with trying to convince others that our perspective is right and theirs is wrong, or, at best, lacking than we are with consciously making an effort to understand someone else's point of view. Considering an opposing point of view as deficient and lacking in thoughtfulness and logic is more commonplace than finding the value in it. Because conventional discussion invites the establishment of separate camps it too often results in unwanted outcomes, such as arguments, diatribes, stalemates, and, at the extreme, violence. Consequently, inclusive, creative thought and action is severely thwarted if not eliminated.

By using the Understanding Process we emerge into dialogue. This way of communicating between two people or in groups fosters mutual respect, openly sharing views and learning deeply about each other's perspectives, beliefs and values. Using this process cultivates a sense of connectedness with each other, even as we differ. As a result dialogue is more likely than debate to generate inspired answers to seemingly intractable problems.

What is the *Debate Culture?*

An additional purpose of this book is to name and illuminate the *Debate Culture*. The Debate Culture feeds and nourishes, and in turn is fed and nourished by, its dominant modus operandi, conventional discussion. When something doesn't have a name, it is as if it doesn't exist. We may feel its impact but not know what it is, where it is coming from, or what, if anything, to do about it. Carbon monoxide is a concrete example of this. It is an odorless, tasteless, invisible gas that is deadly when ingested. Without knowing of its existence, it would seem that living beings die for no apparent reason. By naming it, identifying it by its chemical composition, and discovering where carbon monoxide comes from, we know how to avoid its lethal potential. Thus naming what was previously unidentified makes the invisible visible, thereby opening the door to different options. Similarly, naming the Debate Culture brings it into fuller view and is useful to us in three key ways.

First, it helps us better to see the particular ways in which the Debate Culture pervades and is continuously supported and reinforced in our institutions and customary ways of engaging with each other. Second, this awareness can create the impetus to discover and explore different options, like the Understanding Process. Identifying the assumptions and beliefs inherent in the Debate Culture helps us to question their validity and usefulness, thereby leading us to seek new ways of thinking and interacting. Third, by recognizing that the Debate Culture is the "air we breath," we can understand why it can be so difficult at times to imagine (not to mention actually practice) another, more beneficial way of interacting.

What is the Debate Culture? Let's look at culture first. Generally culture consists of shared patterns of thinking, feeling and behaving that we learn from and reinforce in each other. Culture helps us to determine, within its particular framework of assumptions, what things *mean*; what is real, good, true, right, and of value. There are limitless formal and informal avenues through which this learning and reinforcing occurs; from our homes, to schools, to media, to workplaces, to just everyday, casual interactions. The more steeped we are in a culture, the more invisible it is to us. We are the proverbial fish in the water. As the water is to the fish, so culture is to us.

The framework of the Debate Culture is built with a host of interlocking, invisible assumptions about the way to discover "the truth" and what is right, good and of value, or not. These assumptions encourage and reinforce beliefs and behaviors that place a premium on being right, persuading others, winning, and finding "The" answer.

Within the Debate Culture debate or argument is not reserved for the debate team. It is overvalued, pervasive and easily escalates into diatribes of dubious value. Debate is not particularized and used as a tool for specific purposes in defined contexts. As such to talk with each other is often to engage, in varying degrees, in the Conventional Discussion Process. In this way conversations, especially those in which we have a stake, unwittingly become contests, with all that implies about attacking, defending, winning, and losing.

Dialogue: An Alternative to Debate

At this juncture it is important to emphasize that the Conventional Discussion Process itself can be useful when it is judiciously and appropriately applied, when it is used as a tool with a specific purpose. Indeed the principles of persuasion and debate have roots in the revered works of classical writers such as Aristotle and Cicero. Seeking truth by positing an idea and then challenging its verity is the basis of the scientific method and a central tenet of our system of education. To this point Prince Otto von Bismark is quoted as saying, "To become properly acquainted with the truth we must first have disbelieved it, and disputed against it."

Conventional discussion, per se, is not the issue. The extent to which we unquestioningly accept its value and our habitual use of it is.

Unfortunately we are so steeped in debate, proving one's point and challenging others, that alternative possibilities for interaction are often eclipsed from our view. It is interesting to notice that even when we say we want to dialogue we commonly end up in debate. We appear to have a longing to do something different but the vortex of habit confounds us. As a result our options for building mutual respect, deepening understanding among each other, and creating more beneficial outcomes than we experience currently are severely limited. We tend to be on automatic-pilot, to lapse into some form of debate even when it is disadvantageous or destructive to do so. This book invites you to broaden your repertoire, to learn and practice an alternative framework and approach.

In contrast the Understanding Process creates and nourishes a self-reinforcing atmosphere of exploration, discovery and trust. New options and possibilities appear on the horizon as understanding deepens and insights crystallize. Often disagreements recede in importance, and either disappear altogether or transform into opportunities for innovation. Relationships are frequently discovered among seemingly unrelated things. Participating together in this spirit of discovery by being open to what's new and valuable (especially, in that which is unfamiliar or disagreeable) is an essential aspect of dialogue as distinguished from debate. The Understanding Process guides us there.

Understanding Process: Technique or Living Technology?

Whether we approach the Understanding Process as a *technique* or a *living technology* determines how far it can take us. Thought of and used merely as a technique, dialogue provides a valuable alternative and offers some relief from the consequences of destructive debate. Situationally it also helps to produce better outcomes.

Engaging with the Understanding Process as a living technology can potentially lead us out of the debate frame-of-mind and into something entirely different. We can learn to value, reward and reinforce modes of thinking and behavior embodied in the Understanding Process. Utilizing the Understanding Process as a living technology is explored in Chapter 3.

Many aspects of the Understanding Process that you may be familiar with include: understanding others, listening deeply, suspending judgment, walking in another person's shoes, uncovering and examining assumptions, and dialogue. Numerous ancient philosophies and wisdom traditions, as well as contemporary schools of thought, recommend these concepts and behaviors as being fundamental to deepening self-awareness, positively transforming relationships and organizations, discovering shared meanings while honoring differences, and collaborating insightfully.[2] They also invite us to be open to the creative potential in unanticipated outcomes.

The Understanding Process makes a unique contribution by interweaving many strands of familiar wisdom into a concise, cohesive, "user-friendly" format that delivers results for those who apply it diligently. Chapter 2 explores each of the individual threads and how they interlace together.

The approach we will take to learning the Understanding Process is based on the principle that learning is enhanced and accelerated when we "start from where we are" with what is most familiar and habitual. Because we have been socialized within the Debate Culture, many of us are quite familiar with debate and persuasion whether or not we have been formally trained in it. It feels familiar to us. It's what we have come to expect of ourselves and each other when we are trying to convince someone else, or they us. We are less accustomed to non-critically exploring unfamiliar (or objectionable) ideas from different perspectives or consciously making an effort to understand another person from their point of view. If you are wondering about this, ask yourself "How often have I experienced being listened to without being judged, and even if not agreed with, deeply understood from the standpoint of my own perspective, my own truth?"

We learn the Understanding Process by first becoming aware of the subtle and obvious ways in which we habitually fall into debate. Becoming aware that we are planning our rebuttal when someone else is speaking, for example, is a step toward entering into dialogue. Consciously recognizing what we are doing is the platform from which we can launch ourselves into choosing to do something different. We will learn to listen deeply and calmly with a sense of respectful curiosity as we come to know and truly understand others and ourselves.

It is important to recognize the Understanding Process is just that, a process—not a program. A process addresses *how* we do what we do, whereas a program focuses on content, or *what* we do.

Examples of programs include teambuilding, strategic planning and conflict resolution. The same process can be applied in many different programs. Practicing the Understanding Process greatly enhances the value and effectiveness of programs by providing us with a method for expanding our horizons beyond the Debate Culture on two related fronts, *how we think* and, therefore, *how we relate to each other and ourselves.*

A key to practicing the Understanding Process is the knowledge that understanding someone from their point of view does not necessarily mean agreeing with them. Nor does deeply understanding another perspective require we surrender our own beliefs and values.

How Did the Understanding Process Come About?

Let's take a brief look at the origins of the Understanding Process. By noting what inspired the creation of the Understanding Process, the benefits of using it will become clear.

About a decade ago, in my work as a consultant to corporations and as a university instructor, I noticed the emergence of two related concerns. One is the chronically quarrelsome nature of people's interactions with each other, especially in the face of sensitive and controversial issues. The other is how this debate destructively solidifies the positions taken by people and ruptures relationships. This creates rigid people and organizations that cannot respond spontaneously, creatively and flexibly to new and sometimes chaotic events.

The Debate Culture is widespread and running amuck. In classrooms, training seminars, public arenas, editorial pages, talk radio and television shows, and more recently on the Internet, there appears to be a growing unwillingness to grapple with complexity and ambiguity. Instead, people tend to stake out a clear-cut position on one end of a spectrum in stark opposition to the other end. Considering new information that could lead to reexamining one's initial judgment is seen as a weakness to be avoided at all costs.

As a result too many of our private and public conversations are characterized by knee-jerk judgmentalism, destructive contentiousness, polarized and rigid positions, and an unwillingness to inquire into differences of opinion. We also seem to be at a loss as to how to advocate our own points of view from the standpoint of being partners rather than adversaries. It is not uncommon for discussions to become polarized and deteriorate to name calling and negative labeling. This often leads to an attitude of, "You are either for me or against me. If you're against me, you're wrong. If you're wrong, you're bad. Therefore, you deserve what you get." Destructive debate is rampageous.

In such a climate wholesale criticism is confused with intelligence, and cynicism is mistaken for wisdom. The more critical one can be of an idea or a person, the smarter and more incisive one appears. Assuming a stance of wide-spread suspicion and distrust is seen as a kind of enlightened clearheadedness. Furthermore destroying the reputation of those with whom one disagrees apparently entitles the victor to claim the moral high ground. By so doing, one's position, "I am right and good, and you are wrong and bad," is reaffirmed and solidified.

In the public arena many TV and radio talk programs do an excellent job of fostering and perpetuating these most destructive aspects of the Debate Culture. A significant number of popular "legitimate" news-related programs as well as afternoon talk shows set up gladiatorial-like formats. People with opposing views are pitted against each other and encouraged to fight it out. The less they listen to one another, the more they interrupt, the louder they shout, and the more polarized their views become, presumably, the more "successful" the program is. Some talkshows thrive on putting people with controversial lifestyles or opinions on stage to be pilloried. It is only a slight exaggeration to observe that just as the citizens of Rome flocked to the Coliseum for bloody gladiatorial contests the emperors generously staged for their entertainment, so many of us today routinely attend our modern day versions of "the games," provided for our "education" and entertainment by the media, when we tune into our televisions and radios.

It is an understatement to say that this atmosphere squelches dialogue. It also deadens our spirits by breeding cynicism. Opportunities to discover and learn are tragically forfeited, perhaps forever. Our ability to inquire into what is of value is dulled. Our willingness to "see the other" or "experience the other side"[3] is thwarted if not totally extinguished. These conditions certainly do not encourage and reward understanding about what things mean to someone else from their point of view. On the contrary, openly inquiring into how our own opinions and beliefs appear from the standpoint of others is seen as a sign of weakness and vulnerability rather than strength and integrity. Willingly investigating our own deeply held assumptions is considered heretical by those who hold and identify with the same view. In the Debate Culture we come to believe that the only way to be safe and smart is to play our cards very close to our chests, so close that we often can't see them ourselves.

From an organizational standpoint the prevalence of this kind of behavior throughout an organization or within sub-groups typifies systems that are contracted, rigid and closed. Many systems such as corporations, schools, government agencies, and families are bombarded with new and sometimes unsettling input that creates disorder. People are searching for ways to learn and respond to change more quickly. Despite our best intentions, we unfortunately court failure by embracing thinking and relational processes that promote intransigence.

Despite all of this there are rare moments when something else happens, when people relate with each other in ways uncustomary to the Debate Culture. For example, there are times when:

- **People with strong differences relate to each other honestly and respectfully;**
- **Lasting and meaningful change occurs;**
- **"Sacred" assumptions are openly and non-defensively explored;**
- **People relate to each other as unique and complex human beings;**
- **The seemingly unspeakable is spoken and heard by others;**
- **People seek to deeply understand multiple and conflicting opinions and ideas;**

- People stay connected with each other, even as they differ;
- Compassion and understanding—not necessarily agreement or approval—displace animosity; and
- The universe of possible, positive actions expands.

What is going on when these things happen? Is there a way to deliberately create the likelihood of these things happening? What is necessary to support behavior that creates these outcomes? These are the questions that inspired the development of the Understanding Process that was, and continues to be, nourished by an ongoing dialogue between experience and theory.[4]

In 1990 I inaugurated the Understanding Process with a Fortune 100 high-tech company. I had completed a comprehensive assessment of gender-related issues in the workplace. Generally speaking the data revealed that women and men, by their own accounts, were having very different experiences in the company. Gender differences were especially noteworthy in career development, as was the extent to which people felt included as valued contributors and colleagues. Women overall felt more excluded and less valued than did the men.

As their business consultant I knew the greatest value would be gained from the assessment results if people approached the findings with open minds (and hearts). During the data feedback sessions, if employees could engage each other with genuine curiosity about how it is that women and men were having such different experiences, they could rediscover their organization through each other's eyes. From this vantage point everyone could participate in designing a mutually rewarding future.

I did not want the participants to get into a debate about who's right, who's wrong and who's to blame. If they had, people would likely have become more deeply entrenched in their positions and been unwilling to compromise, much less collaborate. A seaworthy craft was needed that would deliver them to the beaches of dialogue without getting shipwrecked on the rocky shores of divisive debate. The Understanding Process proved to be that seaworthy craft.

The Understanding Process is fundamentally an interaction process that can be applied in a wide range of settings. Since its inception, it has been used effectively in a variety of different contexts, such as:

- teambuilding,
- classrooms,
- counseling,
- decision making, and
- diversity seminars.

In Part II: Applications, we will explore how to apply the Understanding Process in four different contexts.

Why Do We Need to Know and Use the Understanding Process?

People continue to be concerned with the quality of their relationships and organizations, and the character of our public conversations. We are in the midst of contemporary tensions whether due to: rapid changes, increased awareness of diversity and differences, information overload, and doing more and doing it better with fewer resources and less time. As a result people are questioning the lack of civility in collective communication; how we live, talk and work together, and the effectiveness of our solutions and organizations. Scholars and journalists, among others, have expressed concern out about how we regard each other. Here are some recent examples:

Linda Chavez in *USA Today* observed:
There seems to be a growing tendency to portray our political opponents not only as wrong but evil...Politicians poison the debate when they turn policy differences into attacks on their opponents' character, ethics, patriotism and morality. What's more they make legitimate compromise more difficult—and public cynicism inevitable.[5]

William Raspberry of the *Washington Post* commented:
I hear arguments over school choice and campaign finances and tax cuts and welfare reform, and I listen in vain for any hint that the partisans are capable of stepping back from their

group interest to see a fuller picture.[6]

Hillary Rodham Clinton in her syndicated column observed:
*Democracy flourishes when individuals are free to express
differing and controversial positions. Democracy flounders
when any one person or group proclaims there is one right
answer to complex issues...Hate begets more hate and can
create a climate of violence in which extremists may get
pushed over the edge to bomb buildings or assassinate prime
ministers...How do we express our strongest views without
resorting to violence in word or deed? That is a question for
all of us to answer.*[7]

Cornel West, a distinguished scholar, offered the following in an
interview:
*It's fairly clear that the gulf is quite deep between black and
white worlds and black and Jewish worlds. Blacks and whites,
blacks and Jews, live in such different worlds and look at the
world through such different lenses. This poses a huge challenge.
We have to cultivate a much deeper understanding of the various
perceptions from the different worlds.*[8]

Also over the past several years national institutes, commissions appointed by the President of the United States, and a
plethora of special projects, organizations and events have sprout-
ed in an effort to address these kinds of concerns.[9]

In addition to the concerns and questions posed above about
our interactions with each other and their consequences in societal
and political arenas, many of us express similar thoughts regarding interpersonal, group or team, and organizational contexts.

In the *interpersonal* context, people are asking:
- How can I talk with someone with whom I strongly
  disagree, while keeping the lines of communication open
  and treating each other respectfully?
- How can I get beyond defending my position without
  giving up my beliefs and values?
- How do I listen to and speak to someone so that positive

change can occur?
- When I am in strong conflict with someone, what can I do to minimize the likelihood of destructive escalation?
- How can I talk with someone so that issues that seem stuck and unworkable become fluid and move forward?

In the context of *groups*, we wonder how to create high-functioning and inclusive workteams, community groups and classrooms:
- How do we engage each other in ways that appreciate and utilize our diversities of experience, perspective and thinking in order to maximize our individual and collective creativity and potential?
- How do we avoid cognitive blind spots so that we do not miss opportunities and misdiagnose problems?
- How can we all find common ground and explore our differences?
- How can we talk together so that all voices are heard and the value in everyone's contribution is recognized?

From an *organizational* standpoint we are asking:
- How can we create and maintain organizations that more easily adapt to constant change?
- How can we lead and participate in organizations where we deliberately seek out, include and benefit from multiple voices and perspectives?
- What skills do we need to create systems that welcome and use seemingly chaotic input as opportunities for development and transformation?
- How can we create organizational cultures that support dialogue by rewarding collaboration, listening, and inquiring into our assumptions about the meaning of things?

Regardless of the situations in which we live, learn and work, the questions above and others like them are surfacing with increasing frequency and urgency. For example, are you:
- Trying to help people stay motivated and engaged in the face of continuous change?

- Seeking to inspire yourself and others to greater heights of satisfaction, meaning and creativity?
- Looking for ways to recognize, include and value all kinds of diversities?
- Seeking ways both to deal substantively with real issues and to improve the civility of our private and public conversations?
- Leading or participating in domestic and/or international diverse workforces or classrooms?
- Marketing to domestically and/or internationally diverse markets?
- Seeking ways to think and act outside of the box?
- Leading or participating in rapid change within your organization, community, marketplace, and the world?
- Creating learning organizations?
- Leading inclusive organizations?
- Creating self-directed workteams?

The Understanding Process can help us to be successful in these endeavors by offering an alternative to the habits we have learned. It is a way to create an environment in which people can talk about anything, no matter how controversial. It facilitates openly sharing views and discovering new possibilities by deeply communicating with each other.

Where before the intent may have been to prove a point and demolish the opposition, with the outcome of dead-ends and dead-locks, mastering the Understanding Process opens worlds of new possibilities.

Inside the Understanding Process

> *To see ourselves as others see us is a most salutary gift.*
> *Hardly less important is the capacity to see others as they see*
> *themselves.*
>
> Aldous Huxley

T he overview of the Understanding Process presented in this chapter is intended to provide a conceptual foundation on which you can build your competency in using it. Because it's easier to learn something new when it is anchored in the familiar, the Conventional Discussion Process (the modus operandi of the Debate Culture) will be used as a springboard for learning about the Understanding Process. Although both describe self-reinforcing processes *about how we think* and *how we relate* with each other (and to ourselves), they cut very different paths to distinctly different outcomes.

The Value of Debate

Before proceeding, I want to again explain that what follows is not a condemnation of the Conventional Discussion Process and its outcome, debate. Essentially the Conventional Discussion Process is based on doubting or accepting nothing at face value by "putting something on trial to see if it is wanting or not."[10] As noted this approach is useful when used appropriately, for example, in the scientific method. This underlying principle is also at the heart of the United States system of justice. In criminal trials, for example, the defense tries to establish reasonable doubt in the prosecution's argument.

The difficulty arises when we habitually use the Conventional

Discussion Process. Because it is familiar and has been useful in some circumstances, it becomes like the proverbial hammer. If the hammer is the tool to which we are most accustomed, everything is seen as being a nail in need of a hammer. Have you ever had the experience of casually talking with someone about something that seems to be inconsequential only to have it turn into a subtle tug-of-war? For example, you tell a friend where you went to lunch and that you enjoyed eating there. They reply with, "That place is terrible, I've never had a good meal there." Perhaps you begin to wonder if they are criticizing your knowledge about quality food and restaurants, something in which you take pride. You reply, "You probably were there on an 'off' day, but that is one of the better places in town. The meals and service are consistently good." And so on. There is no big calamity here, just the lingering feeling that something seemed out-of-sync.

Another factor that reinforces our tendency to unthinkingly use the Conventional Discussion Process, as noted earlier, is the extent to which we are exposed to it through the media. From talk radio to TV tell-it-all talk shows to print news, the Conventional Discussion Process is the favored mode of interaction. Although there are a few notable exceptions, generally winning the argument and having the last word is more highly valued than understanding the various points of view that people bring to the table. As a result we rarely experience thoughtful conversation about a point of view and how it is seen and understood from other perspectives. Often I have wished a commentator would simply say, "Tell us more about what you mean." Or, "If I understand what you're saying, you're most concerned about privacy rights. Others focus primarily on what they see are the moral issues involved. From your standpoint, help our listeners understand your views on the moral aspect of these issues and how you see their relationship to privacy concerns."

Is There a Place for Critical Thinking in the Understanding Process?

By now you may be wondering whether or not there is room for *critical thinking* in the Understanding Process. The answer is a resounding "Yes." It is an integral part if, by critical thinking, we mean carefully *investigating ideas from various points of view and exploring their underlying assumptions.* This approach to critical thinking is distinct from criticizing and judging. Whereas, the latter typically involves faultfinding, focusing attention on weak points (and delighting in pointing them out), the former seeks to do something else. Dialogic critical thinking involves deeply understanding divergent perspectives (and the people that hold them), uncovering the value they have to offer, and exploring the complex relationships among them. This is the cognitive heart of the Understanding Process.

There is a reciprocal relationship between the process of dialogue and critical thinking. Each one reinforces and supports the other. As we will see, the Understanding Process invites us to surface our assumptions, the building blocks of our opinions and perspectives. In a dialogue atmosphere that is accepting rather than faultfinding, ideas flow more easily and our willingness to explore them deeply and non-defensively is heightened. We are inspired to ask insightful, illuminating questions as our understanding deepens. By engaging in this process, we distill the true essence of our own perspectives and express them more clearly. In this way we create opportunities for ongoing discovery and creativity typically denied by searching out and highlighting perceived flaws, the essence of debate.

Inside Understanding and Conventional Discussion

Recall that the outcomes of the Understanding Process and the Conventional Discussion Process are different. Whereas the former leads us into dialogue, the latter more typically fosters debate. So the question is, "How does each process lead to such different outcomes?"

Each process has its own characteristics. The assumptions, mind-sets, behaviors and ultimate goals are quite different. Fundamentally, the Understanding Process is about inquiring into and listening for the stories that give meaning to life for the speaker. We also listen to ourselves in the same spirit in order to apprehend what meaning things truly have for us. By attending to how we think and what we say, feel, believe, and do, we can arrive at a deeper understanding of ourselves and why something is important to us or not. For example, by noticing that you tend to become critical and defensive every time a particular topic comes up, you can inquire into how you are thinking about the issue and your assumptions about it. You can explore what the issue and those who hold strong views about it mean to you, and why you react the way you do.

Underlying the Understanding Process is the assumption that human beings are "meaning makers." We need to find meaning in life and to make sense of our experiences.[11] We do that by interpreting things through the use of language and narratives that implicitly contain within them our most basic assumptions, what we take for granted about what is "true" and "real." That is, we weave stories about how things are or should be, about what things mean to us. We don't necessarily state them outright. In fact, for the most part we can't say what they are because they are so much a part of us that they are invisible to us. Nonetheless, we can choose to pay attention and listen for how we interpret experiences, for what things mean to others and ourselves both in what is spoken and implied.

This chapter will conclude with a brief look at how the behaviors of each process can sometimes appear to be used in service of the other. For example, the Conventional Discussion Process can appear in disguised form as the Understanding Process.

Let's explore the following components of both the Understanding Process and the Conventional Discussion Process:

- The premise;

- The goal;

- The inherent attitude or mental (and feeling) state;

- The focus or what one specifically pays attention to;

- The behaviors including: listening, inquiring and advocating;

- The role one assumes relative to other people; and

- The outcome and culture implications.

The chart on pages 36-37 is an easy reference guide that summarizes the key points in this chapter.

Premise

The Conventional Discussion Process is grounded in the assumption that in any given situation *there is one right perspective or right answer, usually one's own.* From this standpoint, it makes sense that you should try to assert the right answer by persuading others to see things the way you do. Or, if you haven't as yet formed an opinion, you seek out "the" right answer.

The Understanding Process, on the other hand, assumes that there are *multiple, valid perspectives on any given matter, yours included.* No one person or point of view contains the whole "truth" about the matter at hand. Therefore instead of searching for the right answer we explore multiple perspectives, what they mean from different points of view, and the interrelationships among them. As a client delightedly commented,

> *Oh, I get it! It's as if we all have a piece of a large jigsaw puzzle and mistake our piece for the whole puzzle. I argue and debate, trying to convince others that I have the true picture. Using the Understanding Process helps me to see that my piece of the puzzle is both valid and limited. When I get curious and inquire about the other puzzle pieces, other people's perspectives, I see a new, fuller picture.*

As this client observed, each perspective is a different aspect of an overall truth that is found in the interrelationships among the individual pieces. Thinking and conversing in ways that are helpful to discovering such truths are necessarily inclusive in that no point of view is left out arbitrarily or because we disagree with it. This is a complex process that requires restraint. In order to reap its potential we need to "fight the itch for closure."[12] In contrast the premise of the Conventional Discussion Process leads to an exclusive thought and conversational process. Typically we leap to identify the differences among ideas, "scattering them apart." Then we quash the wrong ones in our quest to win, find the right answer and get to closure.

Goal

When using the Understanding Process our goal is to seek deliberately to explore multiple perspectives by *understanding another person or group, from their point of view.* In contrast when we are engaged in the Conventional Discussion Process our goal is *to convince the other person, to win or to be right,* or at least *to find the right answer.* We want to be right and want others to see things from our point of view. That means, of course, that someone loses and is wrong. Needless to say, to win and to be right can feel deliciously righteous! However, despite our apparent victory, the question, "What have I really won?" often doesn't have a very satisfying answer. When you feel like attacking, it's helpful to ponder the words of the Buddha, "In a battle, the winners and the losers both lose."

Sometimes we recognize our desire to win and to be right. At other times, this desire can be very subtle, barely perceptible. Therefore, we need to be self-aware and honest with ourselves about our intentions. Whether or not we are consciously aware of wanting to win or to be right, it can enormously influence the tone and outcome of our interactions. Recall the hypothetical conversation described above regarding the real truth about the quality of a particular restaurant.

Useful questions to ask are:
- In this situation of what value, if any, is it to establish opposing positions that create winners and losers?
- What can be gained, or not, by openly exploring different points of view?
- In what ways can I think and behave that will open, and keep open, the doors to discovery and collaboration?

It's important to know that deeply understanding someone from their own point of view does not necessarily mean agreeing with them. Nor does understanding another perspective require giving up one's own opinions, beliefs and values.

Pulitzer Prize winning playwright, August Wilson, speaks about understanding another person on their own terms without denying or devaluing his own "truth." He was asked how he was able to express the reality of other African Americans whose experiences have been very different from his own. He said:

> *You have to* **listen.** *In the larger society, we are not listening to our kids, black or white. You may have to* **struggle to understand it because it's different from the world you know.** *For instance, if I go and listen to rap, what these kids are doing these days is different from what I did as a teenager, and the way they're working out their social conduct is different from the way we did. So I simply say, 'Okay, I'll buy in on your terms, let me see what's going on with you.'*[13]

August Wilson seeks to understand others on their terms. And, although he acknowledges and honors his own experience as a teenager, he doesn't hold it out as the right or best experience. He doesn't try to convince teens to see things his way, and doesn't put them down when they maintain their own point of view.

Attitude and Focus

Attitude and focus are so closely linked that we will explore them together. *Attitude* refers to the mental position or feeling relative to the person with whom one is interacting. The attitude called for in the Conventional Discussion Process is *evaluating and critical.* The question, *"What's wrong with this picture?"* provides a vehicle to *focus* the attitude of critical evaluation toward what another person or group is saying and doing. Constantly assessing whether we agree with someone or not, whether we like or dislike them and what they say—and if it is stupid or smart, right or wrong—is inherent in our Debate Culture. Not surprisingly how we evaluate ideas, behaviors and people often depends on whether or not we agree with them, or they with us. Our tendency is to judge positively those with whom we agree. Likewise, we are inclined to negatively evaluate those with whom we disagree, or at best, render a neutral opinion.

In contrast the underlying attitude of the Understanding Process is *openness* and *genuine curiosity.* Even if our initial, seemingly automatic response is to notice what is wrong, that perception can be noted and then relegated to the background. In the foreground of our awareness we focus our attention on: *"What's new? Of value? What can I learn?"* Such questions are invitations to attend deliberately to what we don't yet understand. They lead us to inquire about the meaning that ideas, experiences and beliefs hold for people with views and values very different from our own, including those perspectives we find objectionable. These questions also help us to develop an appreciative eye, an eye that searches out novelty and possibility.

Whereas debating and persuading tends to focus our attention narrowly and limit our vision, appreciating multiple perspectives opens the way toward expansiveness and discovery. Indeed, workshop participants commonly remark, "I feel more inclusive and relaxed."

Additionally debate zeroes in on what is wrong, and, by extension, seeks ways to fix or eliminate it. Being aware that you have only one piece of the puzzle allows you to approach conversations with a sense of wonder. There is a willingness to "let be" ideas and people in order to understand them on their own terms. You will be open to discovering other points of view—even if they differ wildly from your own. It is, of course, important to remember that you are not required to agree with or even like what you discover and come to understand.

Behaviors

Three behaviors, *listening, inquiring* and *advocating,* are central to both the Understanding Process and the Conventional Discussion Process. However despite the fact that the behaviors have the same names, they are carried out very differently. Let's take a look.

Listening

When we listen in Understanding Process mode *we accept at face value what another person is saying as being true and real for that individual.* Even if it's contrary to our own beliefs and values, we listen to understand how it makes sense to and has meaning for the speaker. In contrast, when we believe we're right and/or they're wrong we *accept nothing that someone else says at face value.* It is as if we say "No" to all that is heard and proceed to investigate it by taking it apart, piece-by-piece. Again, while this approach may have merit in specific contexts, the kinds of questions we are concerned with are:

- In this instance, does this way of interacting help to build trust, to understand each other, to respectfully explore our differences?
- Does this way of talking help us get to the desired outcome or does it take us further away from where we want to be?

Listening in the Conventional Discussion Process generally means *waiting to talk* and *talking more than we listen.* In those moments when we do have our mouths closed our ears are tuned to uncovering *errors* and *flaws* in what the other person is saying. As they speak we *plan our rebuttal.* Listening is down-time that we use to plan what we are going to say next. For example, while someone else is speaking, have you ever heard your internal voice saying things like: "That's not right. No, no, no, it's not like that, it's like this. That's so stupid I can barely stand to listen to it"? Or perhaps you can recall moments when you tune in and out of the conversation catching just enough of what someone is saying so you can return to the real work at hand, developing your counter argument point-by-point.

In addition to this mental aspect of listening there is often a physical one as well. For example, while "listening" to someone else have you ever noticed a heightened, even agitated, impatient feeling of ready-to-pounce physical energy? Some of us rock slightly back and forth in our seat in a way reminiscent of children who have been told to sit when what they really want to do is go out and play. Rapid head nodding is another common physical expression of this kind of listening. Usually unconscious it conveys not agreement but something like, "Will you get on with it already!"

By contrast when using the Understanding Process we listen *without judgment* or *criticism.* To the extent criticizing is habitual, suspending judgment in this way can be difficult. Furthermore it's tricky to stop doing something—judging, for example—without having something else with which to replace it. Instead of listening judgmentally we can choose to listen to another person with a sense of *wonder* and *curiosity*. To do this it helps to get in touch with the part of ourselves that is curious and willing to understand people from a fresh point of view. Paying attention to people in this way necessarily means that *we listen more than we talk*, and that we *listen for their story*. Listening for someone's story, rather than listening to their story, requires paying close attention to that person. It means respectfully attending to the meanings expressed in what is and is not being said. Being completely present to another person requires giving them your undivided attention.

At this juncture you might be wondering, "If we don't make judgments, how do we know what is right and wrong? How do we make decisions?" I find it useful to draw a distinction between "being judgmental" and making a judgment. Some of us live in a chronic judgmental state of mind. This kind of knee-jerk reaction is harmful to ourselves and each other. It keeps us separate and distant from each other and closes us off from the new and unfamiliar.

On the other hand we need to be able to make judgments when necessary based on values and principled criteria to which we have given careful consideration. This is essential to being ethical and living with integrity and self-respect. The Understanding Process in no way interferes with this. If anything it enhances it by providing us with a means of exploring and clarifying values and beliefs in depth.

Finally what do we do with the positive, negative and neutral reactions we experience internally when we are listening to someone else? We are accustomed to paying more attention and giving more credence to our reactions to what the other person is saying than we do to the other person.

Alternatively we can use our reactions as a signal to ourselves to *reflect* instead of immediately expressing ourselves. Reflecting begins with simply noticing one's reactions without adding additional energy to them. For example, one might become aware that they feel their stomach tighten along with a flash of anger. Rather than fuel the reaction with thoughts like, "I knew it. They are all alike. Stupid and narrow-minded," other options can be chosen. After noting your reaction you can acknowledge to yourself that you have a different point of view from the other person. That's okay, because within the Understanding Process there is no premium placed on agreeing. The point is to acknowledge your reactions, in this case anger and frustration, without letting them undermine your ability to stay present with what is actually going on in the conversation.

Joan Tollifson, in *Bare-Bones Meditation*, describes the challenge our intense reactions present to us. Tollifson, a lesbian, was listening to someone who held strong anti-gay beliefs. She said:

*I hear (what they are saying as) all the anti-gay attitudes and actions that ever existed. I remember the gay people I know who were killed because they were gay...Anti-gay attitudes (particularly in powerful social institutions...) **do** lead to acts that **do** kill people and that came close to killing me.*

*But in actual fact, my life was not threatened by **hearing** (what this person was saying). (My) feelings of hurt and anger and defensiveness made it more difficult to hear accurately what was said...and, this...makes it harder to respond intelligently. Is it possible to see that anti-gay attitudes are hurtful without interpreting them as the deliberate acts of a free agent, aimed at me personally? Hatred...and prejudice don't come out of open listening and love...They come out of conditioning, fear, ignorance and hurt. When we hear them spaciously, with interest and compassion rather than with hatred and blame, it breaks the cycle of violence, attack and defend. It creates space for change. Because when someone thinks I'm an aggressive, mean-spirited jerk, I'm more likely to behave like one. We create each other.*[14]

In the next sections about inquiring and advocating, we will explore how to respond from within the Understanding Process as compared to the Conventional Discussion Process.

Inquiring

When not listening, what are we doing when we are talking? In a nutshell, we are doing some variation of *inquiring* or *advocating*. As is the case with listening, these behaviors look and feel very different from within our two constructs.

Usually, inquiring in the Conventional Discussion Process sounds more like *interrogating*, in which we *ask questions in order to challenge the other person or to support our own position*. Recall that the intention of this process is to convince, win, or be right. Inquiries made in the interest of this goal, no matter how congenial the tone of one's voice, can take on the confrontational quality of a cross-examination. To illustrate this point, let's look at an example from a TV news-talk program. The topic was the medical use of marijuana. One of the moderators who opposed the medical use of marijuana asked a guest to describe his experience of smoking marijuana to quell the nausea of chemotherapy. The guest did and explained how smoking marijuana was the only thing that helped him. The moderator replied, "Your personal testimony is very effective. But you and I both know it's not scientific evidence, don't we?"

On the other hand, the purpose of inquiring can be to ask *questions to deepen understanding about what something means to someone else*. We also inquire in order to *reveal* and *explore assumptions*, both our own and the other person's. Returning to the interchange above, how could the moderator respond using the Understanding Process? She could say, "Your story is very compelling. However I have concerns and questions, and I would like to hear your thoughts about them. I question substituting individual experiences for controlled scientific research, because it can result in medically unqualified conclusions surrounding life and death matters. And to my knowledge there is no scientific evidence supporting the medical use of marijuana. Also, marinol, a form of the active ingredient in marijuana, has been isolated and can be prescribed legally. Did you take marinol and what was your experience with it? Why do you advocate using marijuana rather than marinol?"

Advocating

To advocate means to *recommend* or *maintain* a cause or an idea. At first glance, it is easier to see how advocating is integral to the Conventional Discussion Process, but how does it apply to the Understanding Process? Dialogue is the outcome and its quality and depth hinges to a large degree on participants bringing their whole selves to the interaction. That includes speaking one's truth. Martin Buber, an influential twentieth century philosopher of ethics and religion, is very clear on this point, "If genuine dialogue is to arise, everyone who takes part must bring himself (or herself) into it. And that also means that he (or she) must be willing on each occasion to say what is really in his (or her) mind about the subject of conversation."[15] However Buber goes on to offer a cautionary tale about how quickly life-affirming, true dialogue is killed when advocating (and inquiring) takes on the qualities of debate:

> *I had a friend whom I account as one of the most considerable men of our age. He was a master of conversation, and he loved it, his genuineness as a speaker was evident. But once it happened that he was sitting with two friends...The conversation among the men soon developed into a duel between two of them (I was the third). The other 'duelist'...was (also) a man of true conversation...The friend whom I have called a master of conversation did not speak with his usual composure and strength, but he scintillated, he fought, he triumphed. The dialogue was destroyed.*[16]

Also recall the premise that in any given situation there are multiple, valid answers and perspectives, including one's own. From this standpoint we can offer another point of view in order to deepen understanding of the issues at hand and to learn more about what they mean to someone else, and perhaps to ourselves. By advocating in this way we discover new insights and perspectives, we keep the dialogue alive. For example, combining inquiring and advocacy, one could say, "As I understand you, and let me know if I'm wrong, making sure abortion is safe, legal and available to women is important to you because doing so supports women's bodily integrity, a value that you hold very dear. I share your commitment to valuing women's bodily integrity. However I oppose abortion except under the most extreme of cases, like rape or incest. From my point of view making abortion illegal supports women's bodily integrity because, for example, abortion by its very nature is invasive and destructive to women. Please help me to understand how, for you, making abortion illegal would violate women's bodily integrity."

In contrast the aim of advocating and inquiring in the Conventional Discussion Process is not to deepen understanding, but to reinforce our own position, ultimately to triumph. Indeed from this standpoint it would not be smart to open the door to discovery unless we knew ahead of time what was behind the door and how to "attack it" if it got out. Thus advocating involves *asserting our own position, challenging the other person's evidence and proof,* and *justifying our position and/or ourselves.* And our own assumptions are taken as self-evident truths to be defended, not presuppositions to be openly examined. The other person's assumptions are, however, fair game. Exposing limits, distortions and inaccuracies of their assumptions are useful ways of advocating our position. Undermining the other person's assumptions reinforces the rightness of our own position.

Given this nature of advocacy and inquiry let's revisit the previous example and see what it might look like: "No. You're wrong. Legal abortion does not support women's bodily integrity. You don't even know what bodily integrity means. You think it means a woman can do anything she wants with her body, but it really means not violating her own body, which abortion most certainly does. Making abortions illegal supports women's bodily integrity. Even a child can see this."

A more polite version might sound like this: "I'm sorry to say that legal abortion does not support women's bodily integrity as you claim. Actually abortion does just the opposite, it demeans women. Making abortion illegal would truly support the physical integrity of women because by so doing women and their bodies are honored and respected as being inviolate creators of life. It's as clear as can be."

It is important to note that the Conventional Discussion Process can be done very politely. It does not require put-downs or sarcasm, although it does invite such behavior. In either case, however, it still fractures and destroys genuine dialogue.

Role

In the Conventional Discussion Process we assume one of two roles, the *devil's advocate* or the *truth sayer*.[17] As the devil's advocate we take an opposing point of view. "No, it's not like that, it's like this." All of us at one time or another have played the role of the devil's advocate. A sure way to increase the energy level in almost any interaction with someone is to take the view opposite to that being expressed. It can be an entertaining party game. Sometimes we play the role of the devil's advocate just for fun; sometimes to try to learn something; and sometimes because we feel strongly about defending a belief. Some of us always play the devil's advocate; in other words, it's our style. People for whom playing the devil's advocate is a habit may find themselves locked into debates, falling into arguments and wondering how they got there. Furthermore to the extent that playing the devil's advocate is a familiar habit, being in the role of *walking in the other person's shoes* may be disconcerting at first. Without the tension and contentiousness of debate it may feel like nothing is happening or that one is losing.

As the truth sayer we are committed to asserting the rightness of our perspective, defending it from attack, and hopefully, convincing others to "see the light" as we do. In this role we genuinely believe in the rightness or superiority of our point of view, unlike the role of the devil's advocate, which does not necessarily require that we believe deeply in what we are arguing for. As a result our stake in being right and persuading others to concede to our perspective is very high. Infused with a sense of urgency we intensify our behaviors to make our case. Although we may feel we are fighting the good fight, undertaking this role can unwittingly lead to feeling trapped. It seems that the more strongly we propound our position the more we feel compelled to persist in order to avoid losing face. Thus, we can find ourselves spiraling into a deeper entrenchment with fewer and fewer avenues for escape.

As with the role of the devil's advocate those who easily adopt the truth sayer role may also find walking in the other person's shoes challenging. From the standpoint of the truth sayer the very act of trying to walk in someone else's shoes can be experienced (or be perceived by others) as surrendering the rightness and superiority of their beliefs. This, of course, strikes at the very heart of the truth sayer.

In the Understanding Process we walk along side of rather than in opposition to our conversation partner(s). When we walk in someone else's shoes we are trying to understand them from their standpoint, as best we can. We go along with them on the path of their choosing because we want to understand them from inside their experience. We adopt the attitude of an explorer, thriving on discovery, and assuming this role in no way requires us to surrender our own beliefs. In fact the more deeply we know ourselves and the more confidence we have in our own beliefs, the more readily and openly we are able to engage with others around meaningful differences of experience, values and beliefs.

Buber, paraphrased by Freidman, speaks to this very thing,

Experiencing the other side means to feel an event from the side of the person one meets as well as from one's own side. It is an inclusiveness which realizes the other person in the actuality of his being.[18]

At this juncture I want to draw a distinction between what it means *to understand* and *to be understanding*. When we walk in someone else's shoes our intention is to comprehend their circumstances, experiences and worldview. By so doing we may or may not approve of, agree or empathize with what they are saying or doing. The Understanding Process does not require that you give up your circumstances, experiences or worldview in order to deeply comprehend theirs. It does not demand that you be understanding or empathic. Although this may occur and genuinely being in dialogue may make its occurrence more likely, it is not a required outcome.

In contrast, to be understanding connotes making allowances for someone or something. Sometimes being understanding is what's called for. For example, a friend who was going to house-sit for you while you are on your dream vacation, breaks their leg the day before you were to leave on your trip, and is unable to house-sit. Either you don't go on vacation or, at the last minute, try to find someone else. But you don't think of your friend as having betrayed you by breaking an agreement around which you had planned your trip. Indeed you likely feel empathy for the unfortunate plight of your friend and disappointment because of your predicament. You are understanding and make allowances for the change in plans because of the circumstances.

On the other hand being understanding in situations in which it is uncalled for conjures images of martyrdom. For example, let's say that on the day before you are going on vacation, your friend tells you that they have changed their mind; they are unilaterally breaking the agreement. They are not going to house-sit for you because they'd rather do something else. In this instance being understanding would mean making allowances or excuses for your friend leaving you high and dry at this late date. "Oh, never mind, it's okay." This doesn't seem to be respectful of yourself or them.

Interestingly, however, one could still use the Understanding Process in this situation. You could inquire as to how it is possible for your friend to do this with an apparently clear conscience. "Help me to understand this." Also, you could advocate your point of view in the matter by offering your perspective on their behavior and what it means to you. This could be done without digressing into the Conventional Discussion Process in which one of you declares victory over the other. For example, you could say, "As I see it, we had an agreement and you broke it. I'm very disappointed and hurt. I'm also angry and upset. This vacation means a lot to me. I really don't understand how you can break your commitment to me and then tell me I should not be upset about it. Help me to understand this. How do you make sense out of it?"

Outcome

By exploring the above components of both processes, it is easy to see how the two lead to very different outcomes—*debate* and *dialogue*—that support and reinforce very different cultures. Debate can often degenerate into destructive arguments, increasing the polarization between people and groups and solidifying positions. All of this dims the prospects for collaboration and change. It is especially likely to lead to unwelcome outcomes when we use it habitually. At such times we are running on autopilot rather than making skillful choices suited to the situations in which we find ourselves.

Dialogue on the other hand involves intentionally seeking to understand by listening deeply, inquiring and advocating in order to uncover meanings, revealing assumptions, and walking in another person's shoes. Although dialogue is, in and of itself, outcome-free, it can enhance the effectiveness and creativity of our actions. For example, before reaching for a solution, it is helpful to take the time to explore what the problem looks like from each other's points of view. By so doing, a solution that was until now unimaginable can emerge with the support of everyone concerned.

Dialogue is by its nature a two-way street, an unfolding give-and-take as understanding grows. After making the effort to comprehend someone and establish with them that in fact you do, you can extend an invitation to the other person to listen to your perspective. People usually agree willingly. There is no mystery here. Recall a time when you felt truly understood by someone else—deeply understood. Didn't you then feel more willing to listen to what they had to say? Listening deeply to someone is an expression of generosity. Generosity begets generosity. An atmosphere of generosity breeds a sense of abundance, that there is enough for everyone. In such a climate there is less fear and more openness. Our Debate Culture tends to foster a "deficit climate." A deficit climate breeds fear. Often we cope with fear by defending and attacking, which further feeds the atmosphere of fear. In contrast the Understanding Process is more likely to create a climate of plenitude which ushers us into genuine dialogue.

Disguises

It should be noted that the Understanding Process behaviors can be used in the service of the Conventional Discussion Process. For example:

- Arguing so politely and gently it almost seems like understanding;
- Playing "Gotcha," by talking to a person using dialogue behaviors then attacking them after they have disclosed their real feelings;
- Asking critical, judgmental questions using seemingly sensitive language. For example, "Help me to understand how you could have arrived at such an uninformed opinion;" and
- Acting like we are engaged in the Understanding Process but being in a Conventional Discussion Process frame-of-mind. For example, as we quietly listen we focus our attention on uncovering flaws in what the other person is saying.

There are also some ways in which conventional discussion behaviors can be used within the Understanding Process, *provided our intention is truly to understand the other person from their standpoint.* For example, suppose someone claimed smokers are drug addicts who should be condemned and ostracized from the community. From within the Understanding Process, one could ask a devil's advocate-like question, "What if your son smoked and could not stop? I know he is very important to you and you care about him deeply. Help me to understand how you would reconcile your feelings for him and your conviction that smokers should be shunned." This is not an interrogation. The person asking the question is genuinely trying to understand what they see as a conflict between the other person's feelings and beliefs.

The key questions to keep in mind are:

- What is my intention? To win, to be right, to sell, to persuade?
- Am I responding critically and judgmentally?

If so then regardless of your behaviors, you are engaged in the

Conventional Discussion Process and dialogue will be squashed. On the other hand even if you use what looks like Conventional Discussion Process behaviors, you are nonetheless engaged in the Understanding Process if you have *suspended judgment* and your *intention* is to understand someone else, to learn about their perspective, beliefs and values.

Conclusion

Now we have a basic conceptual grasp of both the Understanding Process and the Conventional Discussion Process. We've explored how each leads to different outcomes, dialogue and debate respectively, and we've established that neither one is inherently right or wrong. Rather we need to stay alert to whether or not the process in which we are engaged is working for us and others. Too often we slip into our habits because they are so familiar. Our challenge is to become at least as comfortable and competent with the Understanding Process as we are with the Conventional Discussion Process so that we can intentionally make choices about how we engage with others and ourselves.

In the following chapter we will explore the rewards of accepting this challenge. As we develop our ability to enter into the Understanding Process frame-of-mind and diligently apply it, we and others stand to benefit in many ways.

	CONVENTIONAL DISCUSSION PROCESS
PREMISE:	In any given situation there is one right answer or right perspective, *usually* one's own.
GOAL:	To win, To be right, To sell, persuade or convince
ATTITUDE:	Evaluating & Critical
FOCUS:	"What's wrong with this picture?"

BEHAVIORS:	**LISTENING:**
	• Accept nothing at face value.
	• Hear advocacy as a challenge to be met.
	• Listen judgmentally.
	• Listen for errors and flaws.
	• Plan your rebuttal.
	• Talk more than you listen.
	
	INQUIRING:
	• Interrogate the other person.
	• Ask questions that:
	  • Support your perspective.
	  • Challenge other person's view.
	
	ADVOCATING:
	• Assert own position.
	• Describe flaws in other perspectives.
	• Justify your position.
	• Defend your assumptions as truth.

ROLE:	Devil's Advocate or Truth Sayer
OUTCOME:	**DEBATE**

THE UNDERSTANDING PROCESS

In any given situation there are multiple, valid answers & perspectives, *including* one's own.

To understand the other person from
their point of view
(To understand <u>does not mean</u> to agree)

Curious & Open

"What's new? Of value? What can I learn?"

LISTENING:
- Accept what is said at face value as true for the giver.
- Hear advocacy as an opportunity to deepen understanding.
- Listen:
  - "For" their story.
  - Without judgment.
- Listen more than you talk.
- Reflect instead of react.

INQUIRING:
- Ask questions in order to:
  - Clarify and deepen your understanding.
  - Understand what another's ideas mean to them.
- Explore taken-for-granted assumptions.

ADVOCATING:
- Offer your ideas as yours only.
- Explore alternative points of view.

Walk in Another's Shoes

DIALOGUE

3

Reaping the Rewards of Practice

Practice is everything.
Periander

People come to know and trust the value of the Understanding Process by experiencing it, by putting it to use for themselves. In this chapter we will explore the benefits of consistent application and practice.

Moving from debate to dialogue fundamentally changes the nature of our conversations. This is because when we genuinely engage in the Understanding Process we are interacting out of a mind-set that is entirely different from that of conventional discussion. The latter evaluates, criticizes and structures our interactions as arguments to be won or lost. From the standpoint of dialogue these strategies are not very useful or particularly interesting. Arriving at a judgment about other people or ideas and winning the argument pale in significance to the value gained from deeply understanding others from within their point-of-view. Furthermore embracing the ambiguity inherent in seeing things from multiple perspectives nurtures the possibility of depth, creativity and discovery.

Rewards and Learnings

Through years of practicing the Understanding Process in a variety of different contexts, the following seven key learnings about human interaction and relationships have repeatedly emerged.

I.   Practicing the Understanding Process is essential to realizing its transformative potential.

II. It only takes one: You can make a difference.

III. The need to agree with each other becomes less important the more we practice the Understanding Process.

IV. "Staying with our differences" kindles inspired ideas and actions, and strengthens relationships.

V.   In the presence of genuine understanding, goodwill and collaboration displace judging and blaming.

VI. Using the Understanding Process heightens our courage and confidence to address rather than avoid difficult situations.

VII. Consistent use of the Understanding Process can foster the emergence of a Dialogue Culture.

When we remember and draw inspiration from these key learnings, they enhance our ability both to think and relate to each other effectively in many different and sometimes difficult situations. They are useful pointers that build durable, flexible relationships—the bedrock of healthy, viable families, communities, teams, and organizations. Furthermore these insights remind us that the Understanding Process reveals its greatest benefits to those who practice and embrace it as a living technology. As we apply this living technology it has the potential to continuously reveal insights and learnings.

Let's move on to the seven learnings while keeping in mind that they offer only a glimpse of the benefits diligent practice can bring.

I. Practicing the Understanding Process is essential to realizing its transformative potential.

We commonly assume that if we grasp something intellectually we know all there is to know about it. We confuse the "finger pointing at the moon" (intellectual knowing) for the moon itself. Because the Understanding Process has face validity (it rings true), it is especially easy to assume that if we understand it intellectually we know it. However without sustained, disciplined practice it is impossible to reap the rewards of this method of interaction and conversation. We must engage in it in order to realize its transformative potential. Halting our exploration at intellectual understanding reduces it to a "good idea" or relegates it to the quickly forgotten domain of "guidelines for meetings".

Practicing the Understanding Process requires intentionality and discipline. Staying with it, especially when it becomes difficult and when it would be easier to succumb to habitual attitudes and behaviors, is precisely when it is most advantageous to persevere. In the following interpersonal example, Walt, a client, explains:

I was infuriated with him. Jim, my colleague and chair of the task force, publicly accused me of undermining the success of the project, made his own reckless recommendations, and then ended the meeting and dismissed us. This wasn't the first time this had happened and I was fed up. I felt entitled to 'nail' him. Besides I was right and everyone else knew I was right.

I was within a hair's breadth of launching a self-defensive attack from which I was certain I would emerge victorious, when I stopped. I was getting all geared up inside for doing battle, but I just stopped. I made a conscious choice to shift to the Understanding Process. I was not comfortable with this move at first. I was in no mood for listening and I also wanted that great feeling of a righteous victory. But I'm committed to learning this process and getting all I can from it. I found Jim pacing in his office, and with all the self-discipline I could muster, I asked, 'You're pretty upset. What's going on?' In response Jim launched into an emotionally passionate speech in defense of the truth and superiority of his ideas. This was difficult to listen to. I could have easily heard him as attacking me. But I did my best to understand him and where he was coming from. I mean, how did he see things? What was the internal logic of his point of view? How did he understand the nature of our repeated collisions?

The more I disciplined myself to listen the more my genuine curiosity grew and defensiveness lessened. We talked (probably for the first time ever) about how, from his point of view, I was undermining the project. We also explored my views on what I perceived to be his recklessness. After a while we really saw how things looked from each other's point of view. It was like a whole new universe opened up.

*I also explained to Jim that I did not want him to ever again humiliate me in meetings. We agreed that in the future we would talk things out, not walk out. Since then as he and I use the Understanding Process, **especially when we'd rather not**, our relationship has changed dramatically for the better. Before everything was an issue, we vacillated between walking on egg shells and blasting each other. Now we've built a new foundation of trust that supports our relationship. It's easier to work together. We cut each other some slack now. We never did that before. And the extra bonus is that we are much more creative together.*

The more we *intentionally* practice, the more likely we are to directly experience a transformation in our thinking and in our relationships. Many people feel calmer, more confident, spontaneous, and at ease in situations that previously evoked stress and defensiveness. As our willingness to experience and experiment with the Understanding Process grows, the tendency to unthinkingly slip into the Conventional Discussion Process diminishes. Debate looks less attractive as an all-purpose approach the more we deepen our understanding by internalizing this process and finding our own voice within it. This is not to say that we never use the Conventional Discussion Process. However when we consciously choose how we interact, our relationships are transformed—and inevitably, so are we.

II. It takes only one: You can make a difference.

One unique attribute of the Understanding Process is that it does not require agreement between two people in order for it to be effective. When one person engages this process, a conversation will shift from debate to dialogue. One person can positively change the course of an interaction from a path of polarized positions, to one of understanding and respecting each other as complex human beings.

This vehicle for dialogue is especially potent when someone is *advocating* their point of view as the truth and the person(s) to whom they are talking has the presence of mind to comprehensively *listen*. For example, during a teambuilding activity a participant says to a manager:

Look this is how it is. Always has been. Always will be. You don't care about our heavy workload and the toll it's taking on us and our families. You never have. And you're making excuses while blaming us.

After a long pause one manager leans forward in his chair and replies:

Help me to understand what has been happening that has led you to this conclusion. I really want to know what it's been like for you and what you would like to see managers, like me, do differently.

The manager's sincere inquiry shifts the course of the session from debate to dialogue. Because the manager is willing to listen to the employee even though the message was delivered offensively, it becomes an opportunity to deepen everyone's understanding of the situation.

This is one of the most powerful aspects of the Understanding Process. By changing your goal and behavior, you can positively impact your relationships. It is important to remember that you don't have to be a manager or be in a work situation to use this approach effectively. You can use it with anyone, at anytime regardless of the other person's behavior.

III. *The need to agree with each other becomes less important the more we practice the Understanding Process.*

Understanding is fine, but don't we need to agree with each other in order to really get along?

This question reveals a widely-held, unexamined assumption that in order to get along, we need to agree. When the Understanding Process is practiced over time, in the same context with the same people, this hidden assumption typically comes to light and its validity is questioned.

We discover, for example, that the more energy we put into understanding other people the more our relationships improve. These relationships now grow in respect, trust and openness. People become more comfortable with revealing and exploring their differences as respect, trust and openness develop. Whether people agree with each other or not, they are now more able to value and learn from the ways in which they are different.

Relationships built with the Understanding Process have a strong foundation that can embrace differences and withstand disagreements. On the other hand relationships that are built primarily on agreeing with each other are far more brittle and fragile because the "price of admission" is agreement. This allows little room for change and growth, or for being who we are.

Finally, as we go through the daily routine of our lives, there is usually less we need to agree on than we might think. Certainly there are times we need to reach agreements. Decisions need to be made. However I find it useful to be mindful about when those times are at hand and when they are not. We can ask ourselves periodically: What do we need to be in agreement about? Anything? What can we let go of? And remember it is sometimes difficult to know whether we truly agree or not if we do not fully understand each other.

IV. *"Staying with our differences" kindles inspired ideas and actions, and strengthens relationships.*

Practicing the Understanding Process helps us to stay with our differences long enough to strengthen our relationships and kindle inspired ideas and actions. Before discussing this further let's explore the tension between likeness and difference.

The Tension Between Likeness and Difference

There is an inherent tension between likeness and difference for us as individuals and in groups. Human beings, especially those raised in the Western-European tradition, are both attracted to and repelled by likeness and similarity with others. In some situations sameness with others is comforting, while at other times it feels suffocating. Experiencing ourselves as unique individuals is affirming in some instances, while at other times it is lonely and isolating. We vacillate between wanting to be a part of something and wanting to be an individual with a unique identity.

Groups of people, often unconsciously, develop norms that guide the degree to which its members can be different and still be accepted as a part of the group. In virtually any group context (i.e., families, workteams, networking groups, management teams, social groups, classrooms, or political groups) there is tension between being one's authentic self, in the sense of bringing all of oneself to the table, and conforming to the norms of the group. The question, "What kinds of and degrees of difference can the group tolerate, much less actively embrace?" is always lurking somewhere in the background.

Dealing with differences, or the lack thereof, is inherent in inter-actions with other people. Because of the ambivalence described above, we experience some degree of discomfort when there are no or too few differences, or when too many or the wrong kind of differences surface. Sometimes we are consciously aware of feeling uncomfortable, and other times our sense of disquietude is outside of our conscious awareness. In either case we tend to cycle back and forth between seeking similarity and seeking difference.

What I have observed in decades of working with individuals

and groups is our tendency to react to difficult differences as if they were a *danger zone* and similarities as if they were a *safety zone*. Though we venture out toward differences we beat a hasty retreat to similarity when things feel like they are getting too dicey in the "dangerous difference zone." This is especially true when we anticipate that conflict and/or the loss of connection with others will be the result. Generally there are two paths back to the "similarity safety zone."

One way back to similarity is to "opt for the safe zone of generalities."[19] For example, you are probably familiar with the generalization that *we are all essentially the same*. It can be expressed as, "Talking about these differences only divides us. Let's stay with what we share in common." Such a comment may be comforting to those who are uneasy with the differences at issue. However the remark can be invalidating to those for whom the differences are meaningful and important. Prematurely cutting off the exploration of differences roots individuals deeper in their position, widens the communication gap, and tears at the fabric of the relationship.

A second retreat to the safety zone of commonality is firmly fixed in the Conventional Discussion Process premise: in any given situation there is one right answer or perspective. Typically someone declares the *truth of the matter*. They assert their perspective by trying to convince others to agree with them because they are right. The voices of those who disagree often are silenced by this behavior. Examples of this approach abound in our organizations, communities and public conversations. This route to common ground can trigger overt and covert power struggles.

Despite even well-intentioned desires to find similarity in the midst of diversity, the two paths described above typically do not lead us to authentic common ground. More often than not they lead to *pseudo-similarity*. Pseudo-similarity has the appearance of unity but it is rigid and unstable at its core because too many voices and perspectives have been left out or squelched. Assumptions are treated as truth rather than being explored and reexamined. Opportunities to discover new ways of looking at issues are lost. And where do these silenced voices go? They don't go away. They find another, sometimes destructive, path to expression. Ironically the very stability that is sought by the two paths described above can actually lead to greater discord.

It is important for us to recognize and acknowledge what we share in common. It is equally important for us to consciously recognize the *value of difference*. We sacrifice depth, understanding, inspiration, and creativity when we abandon the effort to recognize and deeply understand our differences. When we retreat to the similarity safety zone, by way of generalities or assertion of the truth, the common ground we think we have found is in fact a "false friend."[20] There is an appearance of togetherness, but it is superficial and insubstantial at its core. Paradoxically, taking the risk of surfacing our differences, and understanding and respecting them, can potentially bring us closer in ways we have not imagined possible. To retreat from exploring our differences is to abandon a rich source of creative inspiration and opportunities to build genuine relationships. Thus "differences need not necessarily be divisions."[21]

The question is, "How can we stay with our differences and explore them without prematurely retreating to pseudo-similarity?" Or, given that we tend to cycle between sameness and difference, "How can we both acknowledge and honor this tendency to cycle back and forth and, by so doing, consciously extend our stays in the dangerous difference zone and explore them productively?" This is where the Understanding Process contributes enormously.

Inspired Ideas and Actions

Truly inspired ideas and actions are more likely to emerge when people enter into inclusive dialogue.

When difficult issues are raised people use insight and awareness to help themselves and others to avoid the traps of false friendship and caricature, misrepresentation or dismissive judgment. When the going gets tough, practicing the Understanding Process helps people to stay connected, to stay in dialogue with each other as they seek to understand their differences. By deeply understanding and accepting the ways in which we are different, we kindle trusting relationships and inspired ideas and actions.

Ironically, it is also the authentic path to discovering our common-alities. A colleague tells a wonderful story that illustrates this learning. Prior to starting his consulting practice several years ago he was an engineer for a multi-national corporation. During a weekly staff meeting (having previously informed his manager) he told his colleagues that he was gay.

People in our group commonly talked with each other about family life, vacations, spouses, children, buying and remodeling their homes, and stuff like that. Of course they invited me into their conversations with the same questions they were casually asking and answering among themselves, like, 'What are your plans for the holidays?' I thought it would be easier for everyone if they knew I was gay. That way our conversations could proceed candidly and comfortably without my having to sound cryptic and evasive as I tried to respond to their questions without revealing that the person I planned my holidays with was a man.

After the initial stunned silence melted, I asked people if they had any questions or comments. I think my comfort with myself and non-defensiveness with them, no matter what they had to say, created an atmosphere that fostered a willingness to under-stand one another rather than critically judge. About fifteen minutes into our dialogue George, a co-worker, spoke up. After a preamble in which he said he had never known anyone who was gay and he wasn't sure how he felt or what he thought, with a genuine lilt of non-judgmental curiosity in his voice, he simply asked, 'What is it like to be gay?'

Among the things I commented on, I explained that there were very few places in our city which marketed to the gay commu-nity and that my friends and I often had to drive for an hour or so to a near-by city for recreation and entertainment. George pondered this for a moment and said he had never thought about it. Trying to walk in my shoes he observed, 'I have three small children. I would be frustrated if there weren't any convenient places that were kid-friendly. We've taken them to nice restaurants that mostly cater to adult couples, and felt very uncomfortable and silently ridiculed.'

As the story turns out that night George talked with his wife, Jean, about me and the group conversation. Apparently he was particularly taken by the absence of recreational opportunities. Upon hearing this Jean, who was the market developer for a public golf course and tennis club, got the inspired idea that perhaps the gay community was a potential market. Soon thereafter Jean started the first gay golf and tennis leagues in our city. Within a year other recreational facilities followed suit. It was a great success for everyone.

I firmly believe that this would not have come about had the conversation at work been conducted in the Conventional Discussion Process mode. I could have behaved defensively, challenging others when they disagreed or felt uncomfortable with my being gay. The situation could have become very tense and polarized. Under such conditions George likely would not have asked the question as innocently as he did. It was George's question that prompted me to reflect on the dearth of public places to socialize. Without his asking it would not have occurred to me to mention it. By seeking to understand each other non-judgmentally, by letting our differences "be" without trying to deny them or find consensus, I think we created a fertile atmosphere for acceptance and creativity. George was able to take his curiosity and thoughts to Jean who saw what he was saying from an entirely different point of view, that of a market developer. And you know the rest.

V. *In the presence of genuine understanding, goodwill and collaboration displace judging and blaming.*

The Understanding Process is a useful tool for transforming destructive attitudes into opportunities for collaboration and relationship building.

Have you ever felt frustrated, critical or blaming? It is easy to make judgments about the person(s) with whom we are

frustrated. For example, "Sam can't do anything right. He's care-
less and irresponsible." Or perhaps we attribute negative motives
to someone with whom we are disgruntled, "Jane is refusing to
respond to requests for information because she is greedy and
wants all the credit for the success of this project."

There are many ways to handle these disturbing situations. For
example, with an air of righteous indignation we can give our
nemesis a piece of our mind. Or we can try to put a lid on our reactions, pretending nothing is bothering us. The problem with these
approaches is that our feelings usually affect our demeanor and
behavior anyway. Of course we always have the option of giving
ourselves the gift of guilt for behaving badly.

The Understanding Process offers an alternative approach.
First, we must acknowledge when we are experiencing anger, frustration, blame, and being critical in a nit-picky sort of way. Second,
we treat this awareness as a gift to ourselves. It is a signal that there
is something about the situation and the person(s) involved that
we do not yet understand as well as we could, from their point of
view. Third, use this reasoning approach with the other person(s)
to gain a deeper understanding.

Usually as we come to truly understand what is going on from
the other person's standpoint, it becomes difficult to maintain a
position of criticism and blame. Blame and criticism recede along
with anger, giving way to a willingness to collaborate on discovering new possibilities for dealing with the situation.

The story of Sharon and Jeff, who worked for the same educational institution, illustrates this point. Sharon was the Director of
Housing and Jeff administered on-campus housing. Although
they did not have much daily contact with each other, Jeff needed
Sharon's approval on various proposals and programs before he
could implement them. Weeks went by without Jeff getting any
response from Sharon on items marked "urgent". Jeff was growing extremely frustrated and critical of Sharon's managerial ability. He was sure she held him in low regard. Why else would she
behave this way? Jeff blamed her for the problems he was having
with his people, who felt their hands were tied because they were
unable to move on new programs.

One day Jeff ran into Sharon in the cafeteria. Jeff was feeling superior, and could have furthered his ego and assumption that Sharon was an incompetent manager by criticizing her abilities. He could have fallen into the trap of confusing being critical for being intelligent. Instead just as he was about to tell her about all the problems she was causing for him, he paused. "Sharon, how are you doing? I haven't heard back from you in weeks and I'm wondering what's happening." She explained that recently she had been notified by the president that her departmental budget was being cut drastically due to lower enrollment. Not only couldn't she approve new programs, she was going to have to cut jobs. Rather than immediately demanding to know if his job was threatened, Jeff asked Sharon what it was like for her to be in this very difficult position. He listened attentively as she talked about how disempowered she felt and how worried she was for her employees. Then Jeff shared some of his frustrations and concerns without blaming or criticizing Sharon. What could have degenerated into an argument with hard feelings resulted in collaborative new ideas about how to handle the situation. They also renewed their support for each other and how to best work together during this trying time. Deep understanding seems to be incompatible with blaming and berating.

VI. Using the Understanding Process heightens our courage and confidence to address, rather than avoid, difficult situations.

Difficult situations are predicaments to which we respond with some measure of reluctance, even fear. Have you ever had the experience of just not being able to listen to what someone has to say, whether they are with you face-to-face or on the radio or television, because you found their views and opinions utterly obnoxious? Or perhaps you have avoided dealing with someone or some group because you know they will most likely attack you in some way. Have you ever predicted that things could only worsen rather than improve if an encounter occurred? Sometimes we dodge certain people and situations because experience has taught us well that such encounters lead only to stressful arguments with nothing to show for it.

Of course the best approach to take to some difficult situations is to avoid dealing with them. The question is, do you choose to avoid them because that is truly the wisest thing to do under the circumstances? Or do you avoid difficult predicaments by default because you don't know what else to do to increase the likelihood of a less destructive, if not a favorable, outcome? In other words are you making a real choice? Without options we feel less effective and more like victims of the vicissitudes of life rather than fully engaged participants.

How does the Understanding Process help us to increase our courage and confidence to choose to step up to, rather than back away from, difficult situations? Let's look at the following example for some answers.

Several years ago I was conducting a "Valuing Diversity Training Program" for a large corporation at one of their manufacturing plants. It was a racially diverse group. Over a third was African-American, about half were white, and the rest of the group was mostly comprised of Latinas and Latinos. The majority of the employees had worked at the plant all of their adult lives. The white and African-American employees' families had lived in this community for generations.

While participants were meeting in small groups to apply their learning to real-life case studies, I was making the rounds to each group to see how they were doing with the activity. As I did I overheard a participant strongly assert that he thought it was wrong for me, a white woman, to "stick up for blacks," although he used far more despicable expressions. He continued his tirade spewing a torrent of racist (and sexist) beliefs.

This was a disconcerting situation. Even though he had not spoken to me directly, I had nonetheless overheard him. I could not deny that he said what he said, nor could I pretend that I hadn't heard it. Neither could I rationalize that because it wasn't spoken to me I had no right or obligation to address him about it. I did. I would have been colluding with him in perpetuating the acceptability of racist and sexist prejudice if I just stood by and did nothing. But what to do?

Prior to my development of and practice with the Understanding Process, my choices in approaching difficult situations were limited. Either I would have done nothing, thereby relegating myself to wallow in "guilt gulch," or confronted him in the Conventional Discussion Process style that probably would have led to his becoming even more deeply entrenched in his position and me in mine. However with the Understanding Process in hand, I had another choice.

Immediately after the small group discussions we took a break. Taking him aside I asked to speak to him about the remarks I overheard him make. In a calm, firm voice, I began by telling him that I had a very different point of view from his. "Nonetheless," I went on, "I'm interested in learning how you came to your view of things. You clearly have some very strong feelings. Can you help me to understand how it is that you think and feel the way you do?" As I said this I could feel my trepidation about approaching him dissipate. Relaxing into my confidence in my ability to handle the situation, genuine curiosity about this man and the unquestioned assumptions on which he built his understanding of the world grew.

What began as a potentially volatile situation dissolved into a conversation as he began to reflect out loud. At one point a quizzical look came over his face as he remarked, "You know, no one has ever asked me about this stuff before."

Interestingly after this conversation he seemed calmer and more willing and able to listen to other participants who had views different from his own. When he did express his opinion he was much less defensive and did not use inflammatory language.

What is it about using the Understanding Process that enhances our courage and confidence to deal with situations we might otherwise unwisely confront aggressively or avoid altogether out of dread rather than choice? Essentially by staying focused on the goal–understanding the other person(s) from their point of view rather than trying to win, be right, sell, or convince someone to adopt your perspective–debating or arguing becomes irrelevant. It's beside the point. For many of us, what saps our courage and confidence is the prospect of differences of opinion creating tension and stirring up uncomfortable emotions. Using an insightful approach allows us to circumvent these struggles. This is because when we attend to understanding someone from within their point of view rather than challenging them and asserting our own views, there is no contest or battle to be won or lost. There is only a human being or group we are trying to understand as best we can. And in this context whether we agree with what we come to understand or not is immaterial.

VII. Consistent use of the Understanding Process can foster the emergence of a Dialogue Culture.

Diligently applying the Understanding Process can influence the emergence of a culture that supports and sustains dialogue rather than reinforcing debate. Although the primary aim of this book is to provide a direct method for engaging in dialogue, it is also important to acknowledge the culture shifting possibilities inherent in practicing the Understanding Process as a living technology.

It is helpful to give a name to the culture that could support and sustain this mode of interaction. I refer to it as the Dialogue Culture. As noted in the first chapter that to which we give a name exists in a way it did not previously. Naming the Debate Culture helps us to see more clearly that in which we are steeped. Naming the water helps the fish to see it. In contrast the value in naming the Dialogue Culture is that it helps us to focus our attention on the latent possibilities. The Dialogue Culture is emergent rather than existent. Naming it helps us to consciously seek out and nourish the signs of its appearance.

How can practicing the Understanding Process as a living technology encourage the emergence of the Dialogue Culture? If culture consists of shared patterns (of thinking, feeling and doing) that we learn from and reinforce in each other, then practicing a new way of interacting can become contagious. By exploring the assumptions underlying the meaning we attribute to things (what is real, good, true, right, and of value), we conceivably can grow and nurture an alternative to Debate Culture habits-of-mind and behavior.

In order for this kind of culture change to occur it is imperative that we attend not only to our interpersonal interactions but to our institutions and systems as well. We need to consider the nature of the culture that is institutionalized in the structures, practices, rules, policies, laws and norms by which any given system operates. We need to inquire into how our systems principally encourage and reinforce conventional discussion or understanding and dialogue. Chapter 8: Transforming Groups into Inclusive, Multi-Disciplinary Teams provides a glimpse of how we can support the emergence of a Dialogue Culture.

Conclusion

An essential message to derive from our exploration of these seven learnings is this: Try the Understanding Process for yourself and find out what learnings unfold for you. Using this interactive method in a variety of different contexts was the source of all of these learnings. Thus the more experientially familiar you become, the more you know the terrain from inside your own experience, the more you will perceive insights into its use and value. Perhaps you will find seven more learnings that contribute to deepening our appreciation of the value of dialogue and the nature of the culture that supports it.

In the next chapter we delve more deeply into the goal of the Understanding Process, to understand the other person from their point of view from within their own experience. We will explore the question, "When we seek to understand, on what specifically should we be focusing our undivided attention?"

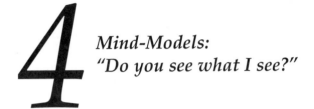

Mind-Models:
"Do you see what I see?"

The way one sees the world depends on one's opinion of it.
The world as one knows it depends on one's perception of it.
Liela Hadley

B ecause deeply understanding other people from their points of view is central to the Understanding Process, let's explore a mechanism called *mind-models* that shapes our experience and strongly influences our perspective. By getting familiar with mind-models, sometimes referred to as filters,[22] schemas,[23] or mental-models,[24] we will gain additional insight into what the goal of the process means in practice. What is it, exactly, that we are seeking to understand? We will also discover how our mind-models can get in the way of our willingness and ability to understand others from within their frame-of-reference.

What are Mind-Models?

It's a cold and snowy morning in Boulder, Colorado. Two feet of snow covered the landscape during the night. Snow continues to fall so heavily that I can barely see the houses on the other side of the street. As I exhume the morning newspaper I hear my neighbor Kevin shoveling his driveway and singing giddily a tune from *Oklahoma* at the top of his lungs, "Oh what a beautiful morning! Oh what a beautiful day!"

Sarah, my six year-old house guest from southern California, who has never seen snow "in person," as she says, pushes past me at the door in nothing more than her nightgown and socks. Before I can grab her to protect her from the cold, she belly flops into the snow shrieking and giggling, apparently oblivious to the freezing wetness enveloping her body. Over my pleas and bargains with Sarah to come into the house only long enough to change into snow boots and warm clothes, I hear yet another neighbor.

Elizabeth is cursing plaintively to herself, "Too damn much snow so early in the season," as she calls for her kids to hurry into the car to leave for school, "NOW!" so she can get to work on time.

Same morning, same snow, very different perceptions. Kevin is part owner of a ski resort. For Kevin, inconveniences brought by the fresh, deep snow, like tire chains and shoveling hundreds of pounds of weighty white wetness, fade into imperceptibility next to the vision of a long and prosperous ski season. Two feet of snow and counting in Boulder can mean at least four feet of glistening powder on the slopes, a magnet for skiers. Sarah sees the snow through cartoon images, the source of her most recent and emotionally charged associations with snow. In her mind she is gallivanting through a white wonderland surrounded by a hundred and one gleeful Dalmatians as they handily escape Cruella's clutches. No wonder she doesn't feel the cold immediately. Elizabeth, an emergency room nurse at the local hospital, sees bloody accidents, injuries and possible death.

In this example, my friends did not experience the snowy morning *directly*, just as it was — cold, wet, white, soft stuff. In fact it is virtually impossible for human beings to directly experience anything. Instead we experience our *mind-models* of things rather than the things themselves. This is what Kevin, Sarah and Elizabeth did. Their experiences of the snow were interpreted through their mind-models of it.

Mind-models are mental mechanisms, "information already in our brains,"[25] we use to attribute meaning to our experiences in order to make sense of them. Considering that in any given moment we are bombarded with massive amounts of stimuli, both internally and externally, our mind-models, ever present and ready, help us to make sense of things by both *sorting* and *interpreting* them. In these ways, our mind-models assist us in meeting our inherently human need to make our experiences meaningful and understandable, a key component in defining culture. They help us to maintain a sense of reality in a way that is relatively consistent and reliable. Margaret Wheatley and Myron Kellner-Rogers address this in their book, *A Simpler Way:*

> *Information relayed from the outside, through our eyes accounts for only 20 percent of what we use to create perception. At least 80 percent of the information that the brain works with is information already in the brain.*

> *We each create our own worlds by what we choose to notice, creating a world...that makes sense to us. We then 'see' the world through this self (or mind-model, in our terms) we have created. Information from the external world is a minor influence.[26]*

Our mind-models operate largely outside of our awareness, and are continuously determining:
- which input we take into account;
- which input we disregard;
- how we evaluate our experience at any give moment—pleasant, unpleasant or neutral;
- what we choose to believe as fact or take on faith;
- what is important to us or center stage in our awareness;
- what we relegate to the background of our mental picture, or consider less important;
- what we omit from our "picture frame" altogether;
- the assumptions or basic truths we hold; and
- the meanings or interpretations we give to our experiences and observations.

It is through our mind-models that we *know* what is real and unreal; good and bad; beautiful and ugly; truth and fiction; valuable and not valuable; desirable and undesirable; possible and impossible.

Returning to Kevin, Sarah and Elizabeth, their unique mind-models shaped their experiences of the same circumstances differently. The interpretations of what this snowy morning "really" meant ranged from potential prosperity, to carefree fantasy and fun, to coping with pain, suffering and loss.

Where Do Mind-Models Come From?

Where do mind-models come from? What contributes to their composition? Why do we assume some things to be true without question? For centuries philosophers, scientists and poets have been pondering these questions. For our purposes these inquires can be addressed by noting and appreciating that our mind-models are fed by an infinite number of tributaries of experiences. Following is a partial list of experiences that feed and nurture the development of our mind-models:

- all prior experiences—remembered and forgotten;
- immutable aspects of ourselves such as age, race, sex, ethnicity;
- religious or spiritual beliefs;
- educational background;
- our families, now and when we were growing up;
- images, dreams and expectations of the future;
- our career/job;
- our hungers, wants and desires;
- health condition;
- socio-economic class, now and when we were growing up;
- sexual orientation;
- familiarity with other cultures;
- travel;
- significant life events: having children, losing a job, marriage or divorce, death and other losses, serious illness, winning the lottery, military service, etc.;
- cultural assumptions, beliefs and values.

The world we construct with our mind-models is the reality we experience. This world is the "real world" for each one of us. Because our mind-models are also the means through which we give meaning to that world, many of us become very emotionally attached to our models of how things are. In fact we become so attached to our mind-models that we forget they are models. We lose sight of the fact that there are many other valid mind-models about the same thing—snow, for example. Our models become facts and the only real truth.

The Debate Culture solidifies this apparently inherent cognitive tendency and provides us with justification for imposing our mind-models on others. Within the Debate Culture framework mind-models are not necessarily perceived as mind-models at all. Since we experience them as "fact" we treat them as fact. When in conventional discussion we impose our facts on others, we are simply imparting the "truth".

Dialogue, in contrast, fosters a lighter touch with our mind-models. In a manner of speaking there is a mind-model about mind-models, about assumptions and points of view, and how to regard them. Rather than impose our model of reality we are encouraged to consider our view as one perspective among many points of view that need to be understood from within their respective mind-models of how things are.

When many people share mind-models about the same thing, such as smoking or nuclear energy, we develop what I call collective consensus mind-models. Culture is also a source of *collective consensus* mind-models. Within the Debate Culture, for example, the assumption that in any given situation there is always one right or best answer is embedded in many of our mind-models.

It can be very reassuring to share collective consensus mind-models with a group of like-minded people. Naturally they provide a feeling of belonging and a focal point around which to form an aspect of our identity. They also give us a sense of certainty. All of these things are important to our well-being.

Without a relatively reliable way to make sense of things, we can flounder in a flood of anxiety. The more emotional investment we have in our mind-models, the more we loathe changing them, even in the face of evidence that clearly contradicts or renders them ineffective. It can feel as if our very survival is intimately linked to the continuing validity of our mind-models, regardless of their accuracy or usefulness. A familiar form of this is "denying the obvious." It is not uncommon, as in the case of alcohol abuse, for a person whose significant other is an alcoholic to refuse to recognize what is obvious to everyone else. Their mind-models of how things *should be*, "I am the sort of person who has relationships only with people who mentally and physically take care of themselves and have self control," prevent them from acknowledging how things actually *are*. To the extent they fear that it would irreparably undermine their ability to maintain their positive self-identity and self-respect, they grasp onto their mind-models as if their lives depended on it. At the extreme to reject their mind-model as being an inaccurate representation of "reality" is to invite psychological disintegration.

Many of us would rather cling to faulty mind-models than change them. We defend our perspective of how things are or should be, especially when we perceive they are under attack. In a manner of speaking our mind-models are as necessary to our emotional and mental well-being as oxygen is to our physical health. If our oxygen supply is threatened or cut off, we can suffer brain damage and die. Likewise when the mind-models to which we are strongly attached are threatened and undermined, it can feel as if our very survival is threatened. This being the case it is no wonder that the Debate Culture is so seductive and we slip so easily into the Conventional Discussion Process. It is perfectly designed to aid us in defending our own mind-models as right and true, while challenging others as being defective and wrong.

However while there is not much we can do to change our biological dependency on oxygen, there are several options with mind-models. Although we need mind-models to make sense of our world, we can change them. We can discard or revise those that are no longer working for us. Often this occurs through shifting our perspective and looking at the same phenomena from a different angle. This is precisely what the Understanding Process, and by extension a Dialogue Culture, supports and reinforces.

Multiple Mind-Models in Action

The realm of human beings interacting with each other is more complex than the wintry scene outside my front door. On that winter morning each person was having their own experience in isolation as their mind-models logically led them. Situations become much more complex, however, when we relate with each other. On the surface it looks straightforward when five people are having a conversation. But imagine what we would see if we had a mind-model recorder that captured the invisible, but often felt, intricate interactions among all of the mind-models that are activated and in play during that five-person conversation. It might be like viewing five different "mind movies" about what was really going on.

To illustrate this complexity and to set the stage for exploring the role of the Understanding Process in cutting through entangled mind-models, let's use a beach ball as an analogy. It is a simple way to talk about a complex phenomenon.[27]

Imagine that you and many other people are all sitting in a circle around a gigantic, multi-colored beach ball. The beach ball is so BIG, that from where you sit *you can see only one color* on the beach ball. Let's say that you see green, Maria sees blue, George sees red, and Michele sees yellow. If I asked, "What color is the ball?" You would say, "Green." Maria would say, "Blue." And so on. But is that true? Of course not, and neither is it false. The color we believe the ball to be depends on two factors:

1. The color we experience from our perspective of the ball; and

2. The mind-model we develop out of that experience, "balls are green," for example.

Of course the mind-model, "balls are green" will influence what we perceive and experience in the future and the meaning we attribute to it. We might not even notice balls that are not green, and if we did, we probably would say that they were not "real balls".

Let's continue with our example. You see green and only green. Your mind-model includes the unquestionable assumption that balls are green. This is completely obvious from your perspective. You decide you want to brighten-up the paint on the ball. You want green paint.[28] Let's say Michele distributes the paint, and you ask her for some. She gives you yellow paint, of course, because her mind-model includes the assumption that "balls are yellow". She feels good about herself because she gave you what she thinks you need. But you want green paint. You tell Michele that she gave you the wrong paint, that you need green paint. She thinks (and maybe says), "I did not give you the wrong paint. I gave you the right paint. The ball is yellow. What's the matter with you? I'm right. You're wrong. You're also ungrateful. You don't need green paint. What are you up to over there anyway? You're going to make a mess of everything."

Since you can't have Michele's experience and you can't live her life, what can you and Michele *do* differently in this predicament? If we want to move toward understanding perspectives different from our own, we need to accept the premise that reality is, like the beach ball, more different colors than any one of us can see from where we sit, more different colors than any of our individual mind-models contain. We need to shift our mind-model about balls from "balls are green" to "balls are multi-colored and this is true even if we see only one color."

Given that we can't have another person's experience, just as they cannot have ours, how can we better understand and communicate effectively with others around the beach ball? How can we help to change the culture from debate to dialogue? Essential to understanding other people is learning to shift our point of view. To do this, we need to temporarily put our own perspective, "balls are green" into the background and focus our attention on Michele's point of view, "balls are yellow". Making this shift does not require that we adopt the belief that "balls are yellow". It does mean that we are willing to entertain this perspective in order to deeply understand the other person from within their frame-of-reference.

> Developing the flexibility of mind necessary to shift out of your own frame-of-reference in order to understand others from within their's is the most fundamental competency necessary for moving out of debate and into understanding and dialogue.

We need to ask ourselves, "Am I willing to be flexible enough to stretch and reach to embrace another person's mind-models, their most basic assumptions, about how things really are whether or not I accept and believe it?"

In order to shift your point of view so that you can understand Michele's mind-models, you would need to:

1. Work from the assumption that the ball is made up of many different colors, not just green.

2. Acknowledge that Michele's experience is different from yours, it's yellow.

3. Be open to learning how she interprets her experience, what experiencing a yellow ball means for her, even if you disagree or disapprove.

Michele, of course, could do the same. Then together you could share your perspectives and explore the relationships among your different experiences and points of view. And keep in mind that you don't have to agree with Michele, or even like her, in order to do this.

Grappling with Power Differences

So far we have been exploring mind-models in the context of fairly equal relationships. What about when there are real power differences? When, paraphrasing George Orwell in the context of our beach ball metaphor, "some colors are more equal than others."

Recall that everyone around this huge beach ball can see only one color. For the purpose of this example, some people have the power, privilege and entitlement to impose their view of the beach ball on others. For example, Randy's side of the ball is orange. From within his mind-model Randy assumes that "orange is what is true, right and good" and "successfully" imposes this view on others around the ball. Where does Randy's power come from? Power such as this can derive from a number of sources, including the following:

Individual Charisma. As an individual, Randy could be powerful and influential because of personal characteristics; he may possess great interpersonal skills and charisma and therefore be able to influence people, positively or negatively.

Position. Randy's power could come from his position in the organization. To the extent that he has control over scarce resources, rewards, knowledge, and access to others with power, he has power and the privileges and entitlements that go along with it. In this case people don't have to like Randy in order for him to exercise his power. His power is tied to his position. If he loses his position, he loses the power and privileges that go with it.

Group "Membership." In a twist on the beach ball image, let's imagine that groups of people, rather than individuals, are clustered around different colors of the ball. Like individuals, these groups can see only their side of the ball, only one color. So there are the Blues, Oranges, Greens, and Yellows. Due to historical, legal, social, economic, and political circumstances and tradition, one group dominates. Let's say the Oranges dominate the ball. As a result they are accustomed to everything working from an Orange perspective, or an Orange consensus mind-model. The whole Beach Ball system, despite all its diversities, functions as if the whole ball were Orange rather than multi-colored. Social customs, laws, distribution of resources, language, beliefs, values, etc., all grow out of an Orange worldview and tend to support Orange interests.

Our friend Randy, being an Orange, derives privileges simply because he is a part of the Orange group. From within Randy's mind-model as an Orange, *his privileges are invisible to him.* In fact rather than privileges, he interprets the benefits of being Orange as rights he earned as an individual and to which he is entitled. It's no wonder that when the Blues and Greens challenge Orange domination of the Beach Ball, Randy and others in his group might feel wrongfully blamed and attacked. Of course from within the Blue and Green consensus mind-model, they are challenging injustice and unfairness. What Randy and other Oranges see as their *rights* the Blues and Greens interpret as "unearned privileges"[29] that are used to silence them and undermine their rights to be heard and taken seriously as esteemed voices of the Beach Ball community.

It is important to point out in our exploration of power and mind-models, that struggles over what things mean can be as vigorously fought as battles over resources, rights and opportunities. In fact disagreements over what things mean and who has the power to define what they mean are often at the root of the other controversies. Humpty Dumpty, in Orange-like, Debate Culture fashion, makes this point clear to Alice:

"I don't know what you mean by 'glory,'" Alice said.

Humpty Dumpty smiled contemptuously. "Of course you don't—till I tell you. I meant 'there's a nice knock-down argument for you!'"

"But 'glory' doesn't mean 'a nice knock-down argument,'" Alice objected.

"When I use a word," Humpty Dumpty said, in a rather scornful tone, "it means just what I choose it to mean— neither more nor less."

"The question is," said Alice, "whether you can make words mean so many different things."

"The question is," said Humpty Dumpty, "which is to be master—that's all."[30]

So where does the Understanding Process fit in? How is it useful for the Oranges? For the Blues and Greens? In this situation there is likely a considerable amount of fear, anger and distrust between the Oranges and the Blues and Greens. Both sides probably have stored up a large supply of negative beliefs and judgments about each other. In other words all parties, from the standpoint of their own mind-models, think they know and understand the other group. While it is true that they have had experiences with each other from which they have drawn conclusions, whether they truly understand each other is doubtful. The Oranges probably have not invested the time and energy to understand the Blues or Greens from *within their frame-of-reference.* And, vice versa. They don't truly understand the nature of each other's mind-models and how their respective experiences have contributed to the different ways in which each group interprets, what is for them, their truth and reality.

When all parties come to perceive that there is possibly some potential benefit to be gained by talking to each other, the Understanding Process provides a way to cut through the judgments and misconceptions. As a general rule it helps if the group with the most power engages in the Understanding Process first. In this instance Orange individuals would practice by listening deeply to the Blues and Greens. This could help considerably to de-escalate the tension. When the Blues and Greens begin to feel more understood than before, they can relate to the Oranges. In this way people come to recognize each other as complex individuals who cannot easily be demonized and reduced to convenient, negative stereotypes. In their place interest and concern grow. These possibilities are the seeds, if tended and nurtured carefully, that could sprout and grow a Dialogue Culture.

Discovering Mind-Models:
Those of Others and Your Own

Remember the goal is to understand another person from their point of view. In light of our exploration of mind-models, this means that when we practice the Understanding Process what we seek to know and understand is another person's mind-models, their (and our) most basic assumptions. We listen deeply for and seek to understand:

• how they interpret events, people and their own experiences;

- what is important to them, of value, and what is not;
- what they assume to be true or not about a given situation; and
- the meaning they ascribe to circumstances.

An assumption I find useful in this endeavor is that there is an *internal logic* to everyone's mind-models, even if that internal logic is not readily apparent to us. Therefore I am paying attention to both learning about someone else's mind-models and how their mind-models hang together in a coherent fashion from their point of view.

So far we have been discovering how to deepen our understanding of other people from their point of view by attending to the mind-models they rely on to make sense of things. In doing this it has been emphasized that understanding someone else on their terms does not require that you agree with them and it does not mean that you have to change your values and beliefs, i.e., your mind-models.

However despite our apparent resistance to exploring and deeply understanding mind-models with which we disagree, we are nonetheless drawn to discovery and change. As mentioned earlier mind-models are not inherently unchangeable, they just appear that way. In fact we are quite capable of revising existing mind-models and creating new ones. One of the ways we begin is by exposing ourselves to what is new and unfamiliar in ways that engage us emotionally and cognitively.

The Understanding Process can be used as a vehicle for revealing, reevaluating and revising our own mind-models. By entering into the mind-models of others while suspending judgment and listening deeply, we inevitably open the door to reexperiencing our own perceptions from the point of view of someone else's mind-models about how things are. We can create the opportunity to discover new perspectives by revealing new doors of perception through which we choose to walk. Michele, for example, could choose not only to understand you and what green means to you, but to get a new perspective on her mind-model, "balls are yellow". She might, as a result, reevaluate her mind-model and discard or revise it. In this way the Understanding Process is a means to dynamic breakthrough, creativity and change.

Recall that the premise underlying the Understanding Process is that there are multiple, valid perspectives on any given issue, including your own. Deliberately setting out to truly understand the variety of mind-models interpreting the issue(s) at hand is useful in two key ways. First, such purposeful inquiry contributes to deepening our understanding of people with perspectives different from our own. Second, understanding other mind-models and using them as mirrors in which to see our own reflections, opens the door to insights and new possibilities that were previously unimaginable. If we do this together well enough and long enough we create real potential for emerging into a Dialogue Culture.

In the next chapter, we will practice with both the Understanding Process and Conventional Discussion Process. By so doing you can experience for yourself the impact of developing a deep understanding of other people's mind-models and your own.

5 Getting Familiar: An Experiential Activity

Listening to others requires quieting some of the voices that already exist within us.

Ram Dass

This chapter takes you through an experiential activity that will give you a feeling for the difference between the Conventional Discussion and Understanding Processes. Regardless of the context in which the Understanding Process eventually will be applied, this activity is a useful and concrete first step in becoming familiar with it. By so doing we lay a foundation for future learning, insight and skill development.

For this activity you will need a partner. It can also be done in a group in which people are in pairs.

Step 1. With your partner or group, brainstorm a list of contentious issues. Encourage people to identify issues that typically spark strong differences of opinion. Record them on a flip chart or notepad so everyone can see them.

For the purpose of this exercise it is beneficial NOT to focus on sensitive, interpersonal issues among the people doing this activity. For example, if the Understanding Process is being introduced in a teambuilding session in which controversial issues between managers and union members will be discussed, don't invite these concerns at this time. Brainstorm a list of issues that are not so personal yet carry a charge for people. The purpose of this activity is to become familiar with and build people's confidence in the process and their ability to use it. It will be applied later in exploring difficult issues, like those between managers and union members.

It is helpful when generating the list, to state a position on a topic rather than describing the topic in general terms. For example, instead of "smoking" say, "smokers should not be able to smoke in the building." Once the ball gets rolling this is very easy to do. Here is a sample list of issues that have been suggested by workshop participants:

- Politicians are all cheats and can't be trusted.
- Our legal systems favors criminals over victims.
- Laws that ban smoking in public places violate the civil rights of people who smoke.
- Gay and lesbian marriages should be legal.
- Older workers should retire and make room for younger people who need jobs.

Step 2. Between you and your partner, or in a group that has been organized into pairs, decide who in the pair will speak first. Whoever speaks first (Person #1) gets to select the topic from the list that will become the focus of the conversation. Person #1 picks a topic they feel strongly about. If their position is the opposite of what was stated during the brainstorming, that's okay. For example, one may feel strongly that gays and lesbians should not be able to be legally married (4th bullet above).

Step 3. Person #1 begins. They state their point of view strongly with all the conviction they feel to Person #2.

Person #2 responds in Conventional Discussion Process mode. If Person #2 happens to agree with what Person #1 is saying, don't let mere agreement get in the way. Play the role of the *devil's advocate* by taking the opposite view. Remember, the intention is to win or be right.

Just in case you would like some additional pointers, here are some things you can do in the role of the devil's advocate in the Conventional Discussion mode. This is by no means a complete list. Can you think of other things you could do?

DOING THE CONVENTIONAL DISCUSSION PROCESS
How to Accept Nothing at Face Value

- Trivialize: make light of what they are saying.
- Challenge all of their so-called "facts".
- Tell them they don't have enough data.
- Tell them their data is inadequate.
- Demand more proof.
- Ignore them.
- Discount what they say.
- Ask leading questions, for example, "Oh, so you're one of them, right?"
- Change the subject.
- Find ways to neutralize their opinion, for example, "So what? That happens to everybody."

Interact in this way for about five minutes but not longer than ten minutes.

Step 4. Stop when you reach a good breaking point after five minutes and reflect on your experience for a moment. Talk with each other. If you are in a group invite the participants to tell the group in a word or two what they experienced: frustrated, energized, intense, or lost interest in talking, etc.

Step 5. Person #1 will begin again with the same topic. Person #1 once again forcefully states their opinions, thoughts and feelings on the same topic. But this time, Person #2 responds using the Understanding Process. That means Person #2 needs to switch gears. Remember this time your goal is to understand your partner from within his or her frame of reference. You do not have to agree. However if you find that you do agree with them, do not assume that you understand them from within their perspective. Even though you are in agreement you could be agreeing for very different reasons. So stay with the process. Again here is a list of pointers on how to respond to your partner. Can you think of others?

DOING THE UNDERSTANDING PROCESS
How to Walk In Your Partner's Shoes

- Relax and quiet your mind.
- Listen without criticizing.
- Listen with a sense of anticipation and wonder.
- Say, "Help me to understand..." or "Tell me more about that."
- Ask clarifying questions.
- Inquire about how the person arrived at their perspective.
- Listen more than you talk—let their story emerge.
- Check for understanding, "Let me know if I understand what you are saying or not. What I hear is..."
- Ask open-ended, non-leading questions: "How does that work?"

Interact this way for at least five minutes but not longer than ten minutes.

Step 6. Stop when you reach a good breaking point after five minutes and reflect on your experience for a moment.

Step 7. Reverse roles so that both of you have the opportunity to be on the receiving end of both the Conventional Discussion and Understanding Processes. This time Person #2 begins and Person #1 responds first using Conventional Discussion and then, in the second round, in the Understanding Process mode. Choose another topic from the list. When you finish explore your responses and then, if in a large group, report back.

Step 8. Debrief the activity by talking with your partner about these questions:

1. What did you notice about how you felt when you were in the Understanding Process? The Conventional Discussion Process? How were they different?

2. When you were advocating your point of view, what was it like for you when your partner responded in Understanding Process mode?

3. Did you notice any difference in how you felt or thought about your partner when you were in the Conventional Discussion Process compared to the Understanding Process? How did you think and feel about yourself?

4. Which process was more comfortable for you? Why?

5. What did you learn about communicating across differences?

6. What questions do you have about the Conventional Discussion or Understanding Processes?

Conclusion

The more we practice and experiment with the Understanding Process as a *living technology*, the more insight we will develop about ourselves, our relationships and the nuances of human communication. Although practicing the Understanding Process brings rewards, it is not always easy to do. Sometimes it takes courage and patience to stay with it, especially when we are having strong and negative reactions to what someone else is saying. Interestingly it is often in the midst of such trying circumstances that we can reap the greatest benefits.

Next in "Part II: Applications" we will build on the basic knowledge and experience you have gained thus far.

PART II

APPLICATIONS: TRANSFORMING OUR CONVERSATIONS

6 *Transforming Destructive Conflict*

The universe is made up of stories, not atoms.

Muriel Rukyser

I nventive ways of engaging in dialogue and enhancing the quality of our interactions and relationships with each other are continuously being discovered. The Understanding Process has been utilized in:

- teambuilding sessions;
- the classroom in order to enhance the exploration of controversial topics;
- counseling sessions;
- valuing diversity workshops;
- problem-solving and decision-making sessions;
- improving interpersonal relationships;
- a communication framework for community meetings; and
- conducting and analyzing organizational assessments.

In Part II we will explore the following applications of the Understanding Process (all the individual names in each story have been changed):

- Transforming destructive conflict in interpersonal relationships.

- Valuing our diversities.
- Transforming groups into inclusive, multi-disciplinary teams.
- Enhancing civility in our public conversations.

These applications are offered as vehicles to spark your own thinking about creative ways you can use this method both personally and professionally. As you do you might be interested in "listening for" indications that elements of a Dialogue Culture are emerging that could support and nourish the valuing, acceptance and use of the Understanding Process. Before going on it is important to be reminded that from the standpoint of this book such a culture shift is not the defining characteristic of success. Remember, it only takes one. You will be making a difference in your own life and the lives of those around you when you practice the Understanding Process. This is success.

Nonetheless a shift from a Debate to a Dialogue Culture can accompany ongoing diligent, appropriate use of the Understanding Process. In turn it provides a "cultural container" that reinforces the continuing use and development of dialogue as a valued mode of interaction. Recall that culture consists of shared patterns of thinking, feeling and behaving that we learn from and reinforce in each other; that culture helps us to determine, within its particular framework of assumptions, what things mean. There are limitless formal and informal avenues through which this learning and reinforcing occurs. This being the case what are some of the things we can "listen for" as indicators that a new culture might be emerging and in need of deliberate tending if it is to develop into one that supports and rewards dialogue?

Consider the following:
- Are behavioral norms beginning to shift such that people are engaging more consistently in Understanding Process behaviors? Are people listening more, seeking out alternative points of view for the purpose of understanding them, and inquiring into what things mean to each other?
- Are people beginning to notice and question the prevailing reward system? (Essentially rewards are things that are relatively scarce and highly valued in any given system: e.g.,

recognition, money, access to valuable resources, power and influence, respect, promotions.) Are they wondering out loud with each other about whether conventional discussion is overvalued? Are they beginning to explore ways to create reward systems that recognize behaviors and desirable outcomes consistent with the Understanding Process?

• When the situation arises to bring new people into the system, is the perceived or demonstrated willingness to engage in dialogue, as we have defined it, considered valuable?

These are just a few examples of the kinds of things to pay attention to. They may be very subtle or tentative signals. That is why, if you are interested in fostering a Dialogue Culture, it is important to have your antenna tuned for clues of readiness. By acknowledging them and engaging with each other about them, you can help to foster the emergence of a Dialogue Culture.

Application: Transforming Interpersonal Conflict

This application demonstrates the value of the Understanding Process for dealing with interpersonal disagreements and conflicts. This story also illustrates two key learning points discussed in Chapter 4:

• **It only takes one. You can make a difference.**

• **The need to agree with each other becomes less important the more we practice the Understanding Process.**

This is the story about a difficult but enduring friendship between Dawn and Marie. Dawn, who had attended one of my workshops, told me about Marie and their recurring conflicts. After learning the Understanding Process, Dawn put it to use with Marie. Dawn was so pleased with how much her relationship with Marie improved that she called and told me this story.

Dawn and Marie have had a difficult, love-hate relationship since they met in graduate school over 20 years ago. Although they admired one another, Dawn and Marie regularly had arguments in which they harshly criticized each other. It looked like their relationship had ended for good after a painful falling out. However after a ten-year hiatus, Marie called Dawn and suggested that they rekindle their friendship. Dawn agreed willingly, believing that both she and Marie had changed and grown over the years. Surely, Dawn thought, they would do a better job of getting along than they had in the early days when they were in school and starting their careers.

To rekindle their relationship they decided to attend a professional conference of mutual interest. The conference was held in a glorious natural setting. The weather was perfect. Conference presentations were stimulating. What could go wrong?

After lunch and before the afternoon sessions began, Dawn and Marie decided to take a walk along the beach. They had been walking and talking not more than a few minutes when Marie launched into—what sounded to Dawn like—a tirade against women who go back to work soon after having babies. Without skipping a beat, Dawn, who has very different and strongly held views on the matter, reacted to Marie by hurling an attack. "Marie, you are so judgmental. You don't know what you are talking about. You're resentful because you stopped your career to stay at home with your kids and I didn't. You don't have one fact to back up what you are saying!" And so on. Marie, being no slouch herself, shot back at Dawn in the same mode.

As the tension intensified and the chasm between them deepened, Dawn realized that not only did she have three more days at the conference, but she and Marie also were sharing a room—and a small room at that. Moreover Dawn reported that even though she thought she was well on her way to winning, she wasn't sure exactly what first prize was. Remembering the Understanding Process Dawn shifted from the Conventional Discussion Process. She changed her intention from winning the argument to understanding Marie on her terms. "It was not easy at first," Dawn recalled. "After all I was on a roll fueled by adrenaline." However when Dawn took the initiative to understand Marie, everything turned around.

Remember how important it is to inquire into and listen for the stories that give meaning to life for the speaker. Our *mind-models* are keys to such meaning. Recall that our mind-models are influenced by many things, such as our cultural values and significant life experiences. Another way to think about the Understanding Process is to think of it as a way of discovering the nature of the mind-models through which people perceive their world.

Dawn shifted from her point of view to Marie's in order to understand Marie's mind-models about women, careers, gender roles, and parenting. Dawn genuinely wanted to discover what was important to Marie and why.

Dawn did her best to understand Marie. Why did Marie seem to be so outraged at women who chose to return to work soon after giving birth? What was so troubling to her? Dawn wanted to learn what those women meant to Marie from her point of view. Dawn sought to understand why Marie was speaking with so much conviction. Dawn also reminded herself that understanding Marie on her terms did not mean that she had to agree with Marie or give up her own beliefs and values in order to understand Marie's.

Dawn also shifted her attitude. "Initially I was very judgmental of Marie," she recalled. "Ironically though I thought Marie was the judgmental one and I was open-minded! My judgments about Marie being intellectually sloppy, critical and overreacting fueled both my desire to win and my conviction that I was right." At first it was difficult for Dawn to let go of her judgments. "However," she recalled, "the more I reminded myself to accept at face value what Marie was saying because it was true and real for her, the more genuinely curious I became about what Marie was expressing." Dawn asked Marie to help her to understand why she thought and felt the way she did. As Marie spoke Dawn listened as an ally rather than as an adversary. Dawn recalled, "I wasn't waiting to speak or planning rebuttals. I just listened."

Dawn learned that Marie's convictions were grounded in her experience as a clinical social worker and in her childhood memories as the daughter of a mother who did not work outside of the home.

What started out as a debate or argument soon evolved into a *dialogue*, an unfolding give-and-take as understanding grew. Dawn checked with Marie as to whether or not she did in fact understand what Marie was saying. After establishing that Marie felt understood, Dawn asked Marie if she was open to hearing her thoughts and feelings about the issue. Marie readily agreed.

"Marie and I still don't agree on many things," Dawn explained. "But our disagreements no longer harm our relationship. Rather than avoiding our disagreements, we more often deliberately seek them out. They are opportunities to learn and to get to know each other better." Dawn continued, "I have found that the more I practice the Understanding Process, the more I feel comfortable and confident stepping up to differences and exploring them."

Dawn and Marie discovered first-hand that whereas the Conventional Discussion Process can fuel polarization, avoidance and withdrawal, the Understanding Process almost always fosters a willingness to stay engaged and connected, even in the midst of disagreement and conflict.

Key Learning Points Reviewed

By taking the initiative to use the Understanding Process, Dawn created an open, welcoming climate. Marie was able to offer her point of view without defending herself. Furthermore as a result of being listened to respectfully and feeling understood rather than ridiculed, Marie felt more open to listening to Dawn's opinion. An atmosphere of understanding gradually replaced an argumentative climate. They were building a new foundation on which to rekindle their friendship.

As a result of this interaction Dawn and Marie began to see the rewards of building their relationship on understanding each other rather than insisting on agreement or winning the argument. Prior to this there were no good options for when they disagreed, which was fairly often. They could "pretend" to agree with one another in order to avoid a conflict, or they could verbally duke it out until the one who was "right" prevailed. Neither of these are desirable outcomes, neither creates room in the friendship for Dawn and Marie to relax and be themselves. By using the Understanding Process they are creating a friendship that is far more flexible, durable, interesting, and fun than the one they had before.

7
Bridging the Diversity Divide

Even as we look upon each other from afar, we
are trapped in each other's imaginations.
David Shipler

W hat does "diversity" mean?

Diversity includes a variety of differences among people including and in no way limited to: race, sex, socio-economic status, age, sexual orientation, physical and mental ableness, ethnicity, religious beliefs, marital status, parental status, military experience, education level and specialization, differences in job levels and classifications, and areas of professional specialization (law, finance, construction, marketing).

What's not working?

Our diversity is present explicitly and implicitly in many of our public and private conversations. Issues regarding race, gender, age, sexual orientation, disability, and class (to name only a few) continuously rise to the surface. We need only to look to our recent history for a litany of events and issues that leaped from television screens, radios and the front pages of newspapers into our daily lives. Rodney King, gay marriages, Clarence Thomas and Anita Hill, Tailhook, perceived abuses of the Americans with Disabilities Act, the end of affirmative action in California, immigration laws, the gender integration of the Citadel and Virginia Military Institute, multicultural education, "English Only," Medicare, minimum wage—and this list barely scratches the surface. Despite attempts to avoid or still diversity controversies once and for all, they continuously reappear both as ghosts haunting us from the past, and as monsters belligerently obstructing our path to the future. Unfortunately in our Debate Culture it is all too common for our conversations concerning diversity-related topics to degenerate into diatribes that are characterized by:

- blaming the victim;
- blaming the system and its representatives;
- feelings of guilt and powerlessness;
- feeling completely misunderstood;
- polarization in which people are divided into victim or oppressor groups;
- denial of relative power, privilege and rank and their impact on people;
- disgust, frustration, anger, and rage;
- hopelessness; and
- fear.

For people that have had these experiences whether in "Valuing Diversity" workshops, our homes, casual conversations, policy meetings, classrooms, or public forums, it is no wonder that many of us are reluctant to participate in conversations on diversity issues.

Destructive diversity conflicts are not going away. Why? The answer to this question is complex and needs to take into account problems that exist at multiple levels, such as: the personal, interpersonal, societal, institutional, cultural, economic, and legal contexts. For the moment let's address the question from the standpoint of the personal and interpersonal contexts. Within these contexts a reason diversity clashes persist is because we are not relating to each other about this multifaceted topic and its attendant problems in ways that foster healing. Because we typically engage each other about diversity issues by using the Conventional Discussion Process, we are like mice running on a wheel—running very fast, working very hard, and getting nowhere. How many times have we heard or said, "Why do we have to keep talking about race? We've been talking about it for decades. Can't we just forget the past and get on with it?"

For all the effort and energy spent, little progress seems to have been made in our ability to relate well with each other around these differences. Many people feel spent and exhausted. Others adopt a cynical stance as a means of protecting themselves from past and anticipated future hurt and disappointment. If we were truly getting on with race and other diversity concerns, they would not keep haunting us in the way that they do. Instead people would be more willing to be honest, open, appreciative, and respectful of themselves and each other.

Truly recognizing, understanding and appreciating our diversity and creating inclusive climates in which people are valued and included requires a foundation of deep mutual understanding. We are not going to agree on everything, and we don't have to. However, we do need to deeply understand each other's mind-models—each other's perceptions of how things "really are" and how they "should be".

Instead where diversity is concerned, we often cling tenaciously to our own mind-models as *the truth*. This is because diversity embraces fundamental beliefs, values, individual and group identities, and entire worldviews. Therefore many people experience their mind-models as essential to their survival. Diversity struggles are intense because so much seems to be at stake. With the Conventional Discussion Process as our tool, we craft our case for the truth and dismantle those who oppose us. When persuasion fails we claim victory if we have quashed our opponents into silence.

Diversity Dialogue: How can the Understanding Process Help?

By diligently engaging in the Understanding Process together, we can weave a respectful and safe "container" that supports and sustains dialogue. This will allow us to explore multiple and often conflicting heartfelt perspectives across the range of diversity issues. Individual and collective consensus mind-models about who we are as blacks, whites, women, men, old, and young, and how we see each other can surface and be explored. Such dialogue creates the conditions for authentic healing.

What is Authentic Healing and What are the Conditions That Support It?

Authentic healing occurs when wounds mend in such a way that, at a minimum, full-functioning is attained. At best post-healing functioning surpasses our wildest hopes and expectations of what's possible. There may still be scars. Just as the scars of open-heart surgery remain long after the patient recovers, scars may remain even though the wounds of prejudice and discrimination (suffered in very different ways by victims, perpetrators and witnesses) have healed. The wound that heals no longer festers. It is not leaking its pain and poison into every nook and cranny of our daily lives, reminding us to be vigilant lest the fouled blade of a hurtful word or deed rip at the painful wound again. When true healing occurs the scars that remain are relegated to the realm of memory, albeit unpleasant and painful memories, of what was then and is no longer able to zap and drain our spirits.

Fundamental to such healing is being deeply understood from one's own standpoint, from within the latticework of one's mind-models. Remember we can deeply understand and grasp the internal logic of another person's reality without condoning that person's behavior or agreeing with their beliefs and values. When it comes to healing, being agreed with pales in significance to being and feeling deeply understood from within one's own point of view. Furthermore being understood without judgment, especially by someone who does not agree with us, can create a sense of deep, calm spaciousness. And because we are not being judged or attacked, we don't have to defend ourselves. If we don't have to defend ourselves, we can, for a moment, just be. Such healing moments create openings for self-reflection and even reconsideration of one's own perspectives, if one so chooses. The

Understanding Process, when practiced diligently, forges the crucible in which such healing and transformations can occur.

Example

In the course of using the Understanding Process and applying it within a variety of diversity contexts (i.e., classrooms, workshops, team building sessions) I have had the honor of witnessing profound moments of deep understanding, healing of relationships, and positive shifts in mind-models. The following example is from a diversity workshop that I conducted with a colleague for a large multi-national corporation. All of the names in the following account have been changed. This example reinforces two of the seven key learnings:

- **"Staying with our differences" kindles inspired ideas and actions and strengthens relationships.**

- **In the presence of genuine understanding, goodwill and collaboration displace judging and blaming.**

It was the morning of the second day of a two-day workshop. The first day had been spent working with the group to lay a foundation on which to build during the second and last day of the program. The Understanding Process had been introduced the day before and the group had practiced it the way I described in Chapter 5.

After getting settled and checking-in with everyone to see how they were doing, we showed a couple of videos dealing with race and the different experiences people of various races have on a daily basis. Afterwards we *invited* people (nothing in this workshop was compulsory) to join one of the following seven groups to discuss the movie:

- Black or African-American
- Asian-American
- White or European-American
- Women
- Men

- Mixed race and gender
- Another option of their choosing as long as at least one other person was willing to join.

They were given a series of questions to address, including why they chose the discussion group they did. We also reviewed the Understanding Process and got an agreement from all the groups that they would do their best to practice it during their conversations. After a period of time with people remaining seated in their groups, we facilitated a large group diversity dialogue.

Far more happened during this dialogue than can be presented here. However there were several significant interactions in which people voluntarily shifted from narrow and/or rigid stances to being open to understanding people who thought and felt very differently from themselves. What follows is a description of one account.

Sally, a white female, had spent most of the workshop seated with her arms crossed, slumped in her chair that she had pulled away from the horseshoe formation in which the other participants were sitting. After the videos, she reluctantly joined the women's group, which turned out to be a white women's group because all of the black and Asian women chose to participate in the black and Asian groups.

During the large group dialogue Carol, an African-American woman, talked about how she could not understand whites who could just stand-by and allow blacks and other people of color to be treated so disrespectfully. "It happens right before their eyes. Just like in the videos. It happens to me all the time. I'm either ignored, mistaken for the cleaning lady or assumed to be a shoplifter. All because I'm black. It's even happened here at work, equal opportunity posters and all! I don't get it. You see it. Why don't you do something, say something? Really I want to know. It just doesn't make any sense to me," Carol implored.

This caught Sally's attention. For the first time she sat up straight in her chair, leaned forward and spoke very slowly and deliberately, "Carol, I know you're talking about me. I saw the joke about blacks that was being sent around by e-mail. I just trashed it. I didn't send it to anyone else. What was I supposed to do? But I think you think I'm racist. Well I'm not racist! I don't do those things."

"What *things*?" Carol asked quizzically. "And I'm being totally honest here, I do think whites are racist, all whites, not just you," Carol contended. "And since you asked, you could have sent an e-mail back to the person who sent it telling them it was wrong and not to send that sort of thing around again. You could have reported it. It is against company policy to distribute offensive material by e-mail. But now I'm wondering. When I say 'whites are racist' what do you think I mean by that?"

"Just what it sounds like!" Sally's voice rises and begins to crack. "The KKK, burning crosses and lynching, terrorism. I HATE THAT! I DON'T CONDONE IT! I DON'T DO IT! I don't know anyone who does and, if I did, I would have nothing to do with them. That is ugly and hateful, just plain wrong."

"That's not what I mean. I know you don't do that. What I mean is that as a white person you have a lot of privileges that I don't have because I'm black. Like, for you, that joke was no big deal. It didn't hurt you. It didn't make you wonder if this was a safe place for you, if management knows about this and did nothing and what that might mean. You didn't get distracted from work by it and spend time wondering things like, 'If I say something, will they think I'm overly sensitive and a trouble maker? Will speaking up wreck my chances for promotion?' This wasn't the tenth time for you this week this kind of thing happened here, at the movies, the dry cleaners, or a restaurant. For you it was nothing. You have the luxury of choosing to say something or not. You chose not to without even thinking about it. That's PRIVILEGE. And from my point of view, that's racism."

"Whoa. I never thought of it that way," Sally replied as she dropped her head in thought. After about a minute of still silence and reflection, Sally looked across the room at Carol and responded, "I have a lot of thinking to do. I don't know if I agree that what you're talking about is racism or not. I don't know what I think about it. I don't really understand it. But I do hear you telling me that I have privileges as a white person in this society and in this company that you don't have and that, from your perspective, I have a responsibility to do something when things like that joke in the e-mail happens. Is that right?"

"Yes."

"Are you saying that you don't have a responsibility to do something too? Is it all on me?"

"No. What I'm saying is that if we both do or say something to make this kind of thing stop, it makes it easier and more likely that it will stop. Frankly I get tired of always being the one who sees racist stuff and who is expected to deal with it. Me and other blacks, I mean. What I want, Sally, is for you to see racism and act to stop it. I don't want this to be just my problem. I want you to be morally outraged too. Do you see what I'm saying?"

"I think I'm getting it. This is so weird. It's as if a whole different way of looking at this stuff is coming into focus. It's like I'm seeing something for the first time and I'm not sure just yet what it is I'm looking at."

After a quiet moment of reflection Sally spoke to the floor before gradually raising her eyes to meet Carol's, "I have the answer to the question you asked earlier. My answer anyway. I'm not proud of it. Your question about how whites can see racism all around them and yet do nothing to stop it. First of all we, I mean I, don't see racism, except for the most blatant stuff, you know, like the burning crosses. Carol, what you're talking about, I haven't noticed. I think you are assuming that we, I, see things and deliberately let them go by. I can see how that would be perplexing and very hurtful. But I don't, or haven't seem them. Here's the rub. See if I paid attention to the racist and insensitive things that people did...if I let myself feel what it must be like to experience such disrespectful and humiliating behavior from others over and over, like you said—well—I would be confronted with something I haven't had to deal with before. Like I am now. I could do what's right and risk taking some sort of action, which is really scary. Or feel like crap about myself because I didn't do anything and I know I should have. So you see it's much easier not to see it in the first place."

As Sally paused to collect her thoughts Carol maintained a steady, anticipatory gaze at her.

Sally resumes, "But now, thanks to these videos and this conversation I can't 'not see' as well as I could before. I can't shut it out so easily. I know the stuff that happens is wrong. I just never thought of myself as having any power or responsibility to do anything about it. But you say I do, in part, because I'm white."

"Right," nods Carol.

"Okay let me think this through. If I see something that's wrong and harmful—racist—then I have a responsibility to say or do something. I believe that. I think that's right. So if I don't step up, then not only am I letting someone else down, but I'm letting myself down too. I'm not doing what I know is right." Taking a deep breath, Sally continues, "Okay. As for the e-mail, I know who sent it to me and I am going to talk with him about it."

"When you do, don't pass the buck to me and other blacks," Carol cautioned. "None of this crap about how 'it offends the black people around here.' I don't need you to rescue me. Please, do this for yourself or don't do it at all."

"Don't worry," Sally retorts with a little more spunk in her tone. "I think this is the part I'm getting. The truth is I really didn't like that cartoon. That's why I trashed it. What I didn't see is the impact of my (and other whites) not doing anything more about it. What I'm seeing now is that I need to address this whether there are black people in our company or not. I don't want to be part of a company that lets this kind of stuff go on."

"Good. Thank you, Sally. But you know, I still don't get what's so difficult about this. It seems so obvious to me. But it wasn't to you. You honestly struggled with this. I can see that. So I guess it's not so obvious to whites. I just thought you were all just being racist fools. But now I'm thinking we see things differently because we live in different worlds, sorta. What you haven't experienced you don't know. And since it's the totality of my experience I can't imagine anyone not knowing what I know—I mean it's so obvious. Hmm. I guess this also means that I don't know what I haven't experienced either. We've never talked about our different worlds before, not like this."

This dialogue went on for a while longer. Then, the rest of the group was invited to respond by expressing any shifts in their own understanding of these issues or by making an inquiry to which anyone who wanted to could respond. To help people listen reflectively and not succumb to knee-jerk reactions, the group also agreed to wait 45 seconds after someone spoke before the next person responded. Some of the comments and inquiries that were made follow:

- "I'm really thinking about this 'responsibility' thing now. What does it mean to take responsibility and specifically, what does it mean for me?" (Asian-American woman)
- "I guess I'm thinking about how we use the label 'racist'. Are people racist or are beliefs and behaviors racist?" (African-American man)
- "This is the first time I ever really talked about race, really talked. It scares me a little but I want to keep doing it." (white woman)
- "Are we assuming that discrimination and responsibility for eradicating it only applies to race? Some of the things being talked about happen to me too. I'd like to know what people think." (woman with total blindness)
- "I just want to know if anything is going to change. Does talk like this move anybody to DO something...or is this just talk? If so I think it's a waste of time." (African-American man)
- "This isn't just a black and white thing. What about Asian-Americans and other groups that aren't represented here, like Chicanos and American Indians? I'm sick of being told I'm the 'model minority.' There's also a lot of differences among Asians. My family is Korean. I want to talk about that too." (Asian-American man)

Common to all of the examples, including those that are not represented here, is that using the Understanding Process helped to create a safe context that allowed the group to move more deeply into the issues than they had before. Because of this experience in which not everyone agreed, but most felt understood in ways that they had not previously, their confidence and courage were elevated. Participants felt less fearful of talking through difficult diversity topics. They were developing confidence in their own and each other's ability to listen to, understand and productively engage with widely different views and experiences.

Key Learning Points Reviewed

In this dialogue Carol and Sally "stayed with their differences" regarding the meaning of racism, taking action against it, and who is responsible for taking such action and why. They did not retreat to the safe haven of pseudo-similarity. By so doing they deepened their relationship and Sally was moved to take action that was, for her, inspired. She discovered a place inside of herself from which to combat racism and racial insensitivity that is rooted in her own values and convictions about what is right. In other words she is not taking action in order to win approval or absolution from Carol (or other blacks) or to restore her image as a "good" white person. She is acting because to do otherwise would be an act of self-betrayal.

Also as Carol and Sally made strides in understanding each other, the judging and blaming present at the beginning of this dialogue subsided. It was replaced by greater goodwill and respect for each other. Additionally the entire group potentially benefited from being present to Sally's and Carol's interaction. They witnessed first-hand, perhaps for the first time, a situation in which differences around race were explored productively.

8

Transforming Groups into Inclusive, Multi-Disciplinary Teams

Our behaviors change only if we decide to belong together differently.
Margaret Wheatley and Myron Kellner-Rogers

Increasingly businesses, educational institutions, non-profit organizations, and others are seeking to transform groups of individuals into inclusive, multi-disciplinary teams. This effort hopes to meet the demands of rapidly changing economic and market environments, enhance learning, and improve effectiveness. The trouble is that simply calling a group a team doesn't make it one. What does?

Functioning as an inclusive team requires *interdependent collaboration through communication*. Interdependent collaboration is nourished by mutual trust. It is further supported by membership on the team being a strong enough source of social identity and pride that one is prepared to subordinate one's individual needs to achieving the purpose and goals of the team. Managers are expected to lead by example in helping employees to forge such teams; however this is often easier said than done. According to recent research the most commonly cited reason that four out of every ten newly promoted managers and executives fail at their jobs within 18 months is "failure to build partnerships and teamwork with subordinates and peers." This reason ranked number one with 82% of the respondents.[31]

Most of our organizations embrace some variation of the Debate Culture. Conventional discussion is the modus operandi of Corporate America. It is difficult at best to create and sustain a team environment within the framework of the Conventional Discussion Process. It encourages one-upmanship and invites the polarization of issues because it fosters exclusive "either/or" thinking rather than inclusive "both/and" formulations. This leads to stalemates which can result in profound immobility or limping ahead with people feeling forced to get onboard with ideas in which they have little investment.

The Understanding Process is a powerful aid for managers and self-managed teams alike to use in facilitating the transformation of groups into teams. Let's look at some of the reasons for this:

- **The very premise that there are multiple valid points of view, including one's own, establishes a foundation for interdependence.** This assumption suggests that the best answer, solution, idea, etc., can be found by exploring the various perspectives held by the individual team members. Everyone is important and has a contribution to make.

  Exploring diverse points of view can reap many rewards. One is innovative synthesis. As different assumptions and ideas are examined, entirely new, previously unimagined approaches can emerge. At other times one person's idea may be adopted in its entirety. Even if the team settles on doing what one member thought was best, it is still more likely to be a better outcome because it will have been examined and understood from many viewpoints.

- **Being listened to and understood builds trust and willingness to subordinate one's individual interest to that of team accomplishment .** When we feel heard and understood, even if disagreed with, we also feel respected. When we feel respected and valued by our peers, it is easier to let go of our own agendas in the interest of the greater good, primarily because doing so does not involve the loss of face or self-respect.

- **Teams generate identification for its members.** Typically we identify with those with whom we agree (or those who agree with us), being the winner, or being on the side of the winners. These are unstable supports on which to build team identification; they lead to "group think". Again the Understanding Process is valuable because it provides a framework that does not require agreement, especially pseudo "go-along-to-get-along-agreement." Unlike the Conventional Discussion Process it doesn't result in winners and losers. It does require that different points of view be understood.

  A team that generates identity among its members through mutual understanding of and appreciation for differences, rather than enforced agreement is stronger because it is more flexible and creative.

- **Unpacking assumptions and being willing to reveal and explore one's own and each other's mind-models (see Chapter 4) is fundamental to effective teamwork.**
  For example, assumptions can be revealed by asking questions like: What barriers are in our way? What is the wind at our back on this project? What are our expectations about the outcome and why? If we fail what are the consequences? What will success look like? How will we know success when we see it? The Understanding Process is a valuable method for surfacing and exploring assumptions without falling into the trap of having to assert or defend them as the truth. Once it becomes a debate about the right answer, the essence of the issue is sacrificed to winning the debate, which is usually beside the point of the critical matters at hand.

Example

Despite all of the available advice, it is challenging to function as a well-honed, multi-disciplinary team that embodies all of the characteristics described above. Instead people often fall into the rut of doing the best they can as a collection of individuals grouped together to accomplish a given task. The following example traces the transformation of a group of individuals into an inclusive team with the help of the Understanding Process. It also illustrates the seventh key learning from Chapter 3:

- **Consistent use of the Understanding Process can foster the emergence of a Dialogue Culture.**

A cross-functional team was appointed by upper management to research, design and implement a plan for restructuring how key tasks were completed and checked for quality. Managers and individual contributors from sales, marketing, product development, production, quality assurance, and human resources comprised the team.

Although this group got off to a rousing start, within six months it was clear something was wrong. For example:

- attendance at meetings was inconsistent and falling off;
- people committed to do things and didn't follow through;
- what was accomplished was always done by the same two people; and
- the same issues kept being revisited, even though the group had made decisions about them.

The group was stuck.

After observing one of their meetings it was clear that this group was not meeting the criteria for developing into a team:

- People were not being listened to much less understood from within their own frame of reference. Members rarely asked for clarification in response to what someone had said.
- Winning the point and being right seemed to drive most of the interactions. More often than not when an idea was offered it was either critiqued (rather than explored) or ignored.
- Different perspectives from separate parts of the business were not elicited and explored. Instead the status hierarchy of the company was reenacted. Representatives from quality assurance and human resources were not listened to

at all, and the people from sales, the aspect of the business ranked highest in the pecking order, drove the agenda. Everyone colluded in this.

- People did not take pride in membership, instead there seemed to be a stigma associated with being on the team. Although their managers had approved their participation, few voluntarily told their colleagues that they were appointed to the team.

- Different assumptions and mind-models operating within the group were not recognized much less examined and understood. Unexamined assumptions about what they could and should do and how it would be received by their colleagues in the organization flowed fast and furious. As a result the group was stuck, running in place.

After offering the above observations to them the group agreed that they needed to do things differently if they had any hope of meeting upper management's expectations.

We began by reviewing the Conventional Discussion Process. They recognized themselves in it immediately. A woman from marketing remarked with a tone of relief, "I'm glad to know there is a name for what we are doing with, or is it 'to,' each other. It helps me just to be able to name it."

After some spirited and enlightening conversation about the merits of debate and playing the devil's advocate I asked, "How is this approach working for you? Are you getting the results you want?" The answer was "No."

They agreed to consider an alternative approach to interacting with each other in order to improve results and morale. After introducing the Understanding Process including the "getting familiar" activity, the team decided to systematically incorporate it into their meetings. Their goal was twofold. In addition to becoming skilled as individuals in the new process, they also sought to shift the behavioral operating norms of the group from unconsciously and habitually criticizing and debating, to choicefully entering into dialogue. Using a disciplined, step-by-step process, they focused on developing the following key competencies which they determined were the most critical for them to master in order

to engage in dialogue and get results:
- Listening non-judgmentally and "for" each other's story;
- Reflecting instead of reacting;
- Eliciting multiple perspectives; and
- Inquiring into assumptions and mind-models.

During each of their next five weekly meetings, the team focused on cultivating specific competencies and then weaving them all together. The group agreed to two ground rules intended to facilitate this learning experience. Because attendance had been erratic, people made a contract with each other to attend these five meetings. Without full participation the team would not have been able to accomplish its goals. The other ground rule concerned decision-making. The team agreed not to make any decisions about what action to take during these five learning and laboratory-like meetings. In this way they could concentrate fully on learning the Understanding Process.

Each of the meetings concluded with "review and reflection."[32] During this time the team offered their thoughts about: 1) the ways in which they accomplished the learning objectives for the day and prospective improvements; 2) insights into the Understanding Process; 3) how they were functioning as a team; and 4) their progress with getting results.

The following section briefly describes the team's progression in learning the key competencies. We combined a variety of proven, effective learning tools which may be familiar to you, like the "talking stick." (Whoever holds the talking stick—a marker can be used as the talking stick—holds the floor. They speak uninterrupted and when they are finished they put the stick or marker down and the next person who wants to speak picks it up). Unique to our approach was the customized application of those tools to teach the Understanding Process in a way that met the specific needs of this team as they dealt with real issues.

We began with listening non-judgmentally for each other's stories. Typically in order to listen well we have to slow down the pace of our interactions. We combined two procedures, the "talking stick" and confirming that each person who spoke was understood from within their frame of reference before moving on to the next speaker. The person holding the talking stick held the floor. After speaking and while still in possession of the stick, at least one other person would confirm that the meaning of the speaker's message was understood. Sometimes it was necessary to ask clarifying questions of the speaker before understanding was established, after which the speaker put the stick in the center of the table. Whoever wanted to speak next picked it up and the process continued.

Suspending judgment when people listened to others presented a challenge. How do we not do something that seems to happen automatically inside of our heads without our even having to try? The first step is to simply notice that we are judging. Once we have established that awareness, we can consciously choose to direct our attention elsewhere. We can be curious about what the other person is expressing and deliberately look for what is new and/or of value. During "review and reflection," team members noted several things about suspending judgment. One person observed that the more they concentrated their attention on truly understanding the speaker, the more their tendency toward judgment and criticism waned in influence and significance.

During the next session we combined "reflecting instead of reacting" and "eliciting multiple perspectives." To help the team engage in reflecting we created time for it between speakers. After each person spoke the team was silent for 30 seconds before the next person contributed. This may not seem like a long time, but considering the rapid response rate many of us are accustomed to, especially in our work environments, it was a solid reminder to take a moment and reflect on what was being expressed, the issues before the team, and one's own response to them. During review and reflection people observed that value was added by taking time to reflect. One team member noted, "I think reflecting greatly improved the quality of our work and our ideas. We seemed to be more 'on point' rather than all over the place like we had been."

Utilizing the diversity on the team, by inviting perspectives from people representing different aspects of the business, was completely foreign. The team needed not only to learn how to do this but to consciously think to do it. To facilitate eliciting multiple perspectives and fully understanding them, each member committed to asking twice about a perspective different from that being discussed during the meeting. Since there were eight people on the team, this meant that varied points of view were sought sixteen times during their meeting. One way they did this was to simply ask, "Sally, I'd like to know what your thoughts are. What does this idea look like from a production vantage point?" Another was for people to wonder out loud, "Is there another take on this approach that we are not considering? Is there another standpoint from which to consider this idea?"

Again, during review and reflection insights surfaced. "Not only did we get a better understanding of the task at hand, but I noticed how much better I'm feeling about being on this team. I think it's because I feel respected by the group for the unique perspective I bring to our charge. Also, I enjoyed inviting others to offer their views. I'm actually looking forward to our next meeting!"

Next the team grappled with surfacing and examining assumptions and mind-models. This can be tricky because our mind-models and the assumptions embedded in them are, by their nature, invisible to us. Recall from our earlier discussion that mind-models have both individual and collective aspects. The team was particularly interested in finding a way to become aware of the group's assumptions about the task they were given. They were correctly wary of falling into the trap of "group think".

The team reviewed what it was that upper management wanted them to produce. Then they responded to a series of questions including:

- We know we will have produced what is expected of us when...
- We will be successful if...
- The worst thing that could happen is...
- The rest of the organization sees this team as...
- The real reason management is asking us to do this is...

The team first completed the sentences in a brainstorming format and recorded what people said. Then utilizing what they had been learning so far about listening, non-judgment, eliciting and deeply understanding varied points of view, they revisited their responses with an eye toward identifying the mind-models and taken-for-granted assumptions on which their responses were based. For example, "We will be successful if there is no resistance to the changes we propose," revealed assumptions about, among other things, success being equated with everyone agreeing with what is proposed. Exploring the unlikelihood of unanimous support, this question also surfaced assumptions about the need to be perfect, for the team not to make any mistakes in order to be successful. No wonder the team was immobilized. Perfection, or maintaining the image of perfection, is exhausting and impossible.

As the team progressed, several issues surfaced during review and reflection. One concerned the role of the Understanding Process in decision-making and the other focused on finding common ground. Regarding the former, the team came to the conclusion that while being in dialogue with each other is not the same thing as decision-making, it can aid and enrich decision-making. By setting aside time to listen, understand, explore multiple perspectives, and ferret out assumptions for investigation; it helped the group to make better decisions faster.

Regarding common ground, the team wrestled with the pervasive assumption that they must agree on almost everything in order to move ahead. When this assumption was challenged they made an important discovery. They learned to ask, "Is this something we need to agree about or not? If not how can we have our different experiences and points of view and still be connected as a team?" As they explored these questions they discovered that many, if not most, things that came up in their conversations did not require agreement. They could just have their differences and not need to hide them or get each other to conform to the dominant view. In the past this would have been virtually impossible because the existence of different points of view tended to be framed as opportunities to be right and to convince others to believe the same.

Epilogue

Follow-up with this team revealed that they had been successful in developing new competencies and in changing the group behavioral norms in ways that supported them in both accomplishing their task and in maintaining quality relationships with each other. As they progressed the team became interested in the idea of a Dialogue Culture and how it might be different from operating within the Debate Culture that characterized the organization as a whole. This stimulated a series of conversations in which they seriously considered questions like those mentioned in the introduction to Part II. They began to notice that the behavioral norms of the group were shifting insofar as people were: listening more, seeking out alternative points of view, surfacing and examining assumptions, openly identifying the value in everyone's ideas (even those with which people strongly disagreed), and inquiring into how their team mates were interpreting ideas and events.

Their conversations are generating a number of interesting ideas for institutional change. For example, reviews, which include feedback from peers, subordinates and managers alike, (and influence raises, bonuses and promotions) are being revisited. They are considering including feedback on the ways in which people both practice the Understanding Process and positively (not dogmatically) encourage the emergence of a Dialogue Culture that supports it.

Conclusion

Just as the Understanding Process was adapted to the team-development needs of this group, so it can be adapted to all manner of innovative initiatives including: developing high performance workteams, establishing self-directed workteams, and collaborative leadership. All of these efforts can be enhanced by incorporating the principles and competencies necessary for dialogue.

Key Learning Point Reviewed

Consistently using the Understanding Process, reaping
its rewards, and incorporating it into how people normally
conduct themselves lays the groundwork for the emergence of
a Dialogue Culture. Keeping in mind that a culture consists
of much more than behavioral norms, the team is exploring
ways in which institutional structures, such as reward systems,
can encourage, support and sustain the development of a
Dialogue Culture.

Enhancing Civility in Our Public Conversations

What we really need to do is go to the people, generate communication and be unafraid to listen.

Joanna Macey

As mentioned in the first chapter, over the last several years there has been a call for improving the quality of our public conversations. Public conversations take place in many different forums including: public meetings, classrooms, government councils and legislatures, political campaigns, TV and radio-talk programs. Commissions have been set up nationally and locally to explore questions like: "How can we speak our own truths and inquire into the ideas of others, especially those with whom we disagree, without resorting to gross generalizations, character assassinations, and outright lies?" Our Debate Culture fosters this kind of destructive contention.

Key to enhancing civility in our public conversations about important and often controversial issues is shifting from the preferred mode of interaction within the Debate Culture to the Understanding Process.

Let's visit two public meetings, one in which a moderator introduced the Understanding Process for the group to use during the meeting, and the other in which the key figure in a controversy used it on her own. First, we will learn about a meeting convened in a community that had rallied to investigate the consequences of a toxic waste incinerator that had been operating in their town for over ten years. In the second example we will meet Maria, the director of a human services agency, who decided to meet publicly with the very disgruntled staff and constituency of a satellite office of the agency.

These examples reinforce the following key learnings:

- **Using the Understanding Process heightens our courage and confidence to address rather than avoid difficult situations.**

- **In the presence of genuine understanding, goodwill and collaboration displace judging and blaming.**

Example One

Finally after a decade of struggling for recognition and funds, a community group received a grant to hire faculty from the local college to investigate the health consequences of a toxic waste incinerator that had been operating in their town for about twelve years.

A meeting had been arranged during which the researchers were going to inform the community members in attendance about the research — when it would start, the questions they were going to ask, how they would analyze the data, and when they would report the findings. However Karen, the person in charge of moderating the meeting, had learned that several community members were outraged at the prospect of doing research. They wanted action. They wanted the waste company sued, the site cleaned up, moved out, and compensatory and punitive damages paid to the community.

Karen decided to introduce the Understanding Process to those in attendance and asked if they would agree to use it during their conversations with each other. After she demonstrated some of the differences between the two processes, answered questions, and reassured people that understanding each other did not necessarily mean agreeing, they accepted dialogue as a way to approach the meeting.

Going into the session Karen was apprehensive about the possibility of blaming, polarization, frustration and hopelessness. Much to the contrary, and with her guidance and support, participants took the premise seriously and deliberately sought out different perspectives. Questions like, "Whom haven't we heard from?" "What point of view is missing from our consideration?" "What haven't we thought about?" were asked at first by Karen and eventually by participants as well. Someone even took the step to inquire, "I'd like to hear what a successful outcome would look like from those who want to do research and those who want to take legal action immediately." Naturally agreement was not the order of the day. However deeper understanding, an increased sense of community, and a willingness to explore a legal alternative in addition to continuing with the research did emerge. A spirit of cooperation was fostered by everyone's concerns being heard, engaged with and understood. People left the meeting feeling they were on the same rather than opposing team. Not everyone agreed on the strategy, but they did discover that they shared a deep commitment to the elimination of the toxic waste site and to listening to each other respectfully, especially when they disagreed.

Afterwards Karen reflected,

By using this process we didn't get into the familiar power struggles as much as we usually do. I think that is because for the most part, people felt heard and taken seriously no matter what they had to say. Consequently we didn't need to use, or is it misuse, the substantive issues of toxic waste, research and legal action, as a means of retaliation for feeling ignored, demeaned, excluded, and so on. We didn't do the usual, "If you won't let me have what I want, I'll see to it that you don't get what you want," or "My concerns are being ignored so I will disrupt the meeting in order get my issue heard."

Example Two

Maria had recently been hired as the new director of a human services agency. After going through a year of intense upheaval, the board of directors was delighted and relieved to have hired her. The agency's main office was in the largest city in the county with satellite offices in other communities. The population of the city in which the main office was located differed from the rest of the county. Predominantly white, highly educated, politically liberal, middle to upper-middle class, it had a reputation in the rest of the county for being out of touch with the real world. Another town, in which a satellite office was located, was home to a racially and ethnically diverse population, many of whom earned their livelihoods working on farms and in construction.

Rarely did the previous director visit this satellite office, which was staffed with people who lived in the town. In fact she never spent any time in the town at all. By the time Maria had assumed the director's post, the tension between the home office (including the board of directors) and the satellite office with its contingent of local supporters, had reached the boiling point.

Maria did have doubts about the satellite office since the staff appeared to be more interested in blowing off steam than in working. She and the board were seriously considering closing the office down. Like her predecessor Maria could have adopted the attitude that this episode, just like all the others, would soon blow over with few repercussions for the agency. However instead of repeating the history she had inherited, Maria decided she would rather visit with the satellite office staff and the concerned people in the town. Her genuine curiosity and interest in truly understanding what was going on out-weighed her misgivings. The board of directors reluctantly agreed to the public meeting.

In addition to the political ramifications of the meeting, there were also personal ones for Maria. She was being accused publicly by members of the satellite office community of being a "traitor to her people" because she, as a Latina, had accepted the directorship of this "elitist" agency. From their point of view Maria was doing the bidding of a ruthless board of directors. None of this was made any easier by the knowledge that the news media would be in attendance as well.

Maria's goal for the meeting was to enter into dialogue with those present. She did not want the meeting to degenerate into a debate causing further polarization and entrenchment. Maria was under no illusion that this would be easy. History haunted the present. In a manner of speaking she expected at least as many ghosts from the past as staff and community people to show up. Complex emotions churning within and among everyone could easily erupt. With all of this in mind as she was driving to the meeting, Maria reviewed key aspects of the Understanding Process that she wanted to keep at the forefront of her awareness as she interacted with the participants:

- "I will keep in mind that there are multiple, valid perspectives on any given situation, (including my own) and intentionally seek out and listen respectfully to different points of view."

- Anticipating that her own judgmentalism would be rearing its head as people spoke, Maria reminded herself of a couple of ways to keep it from contaminating the proceedings:

   "When I notice my knee-jerk judgmentalism is in gear, I will shift my attention to my curiosity about what is being expressed and seek to understand more fully."

   "I can recognize my judgmentalism for what it is, assumptions or premature interpretations of people and events. It is not fact. Then with an open and non-defensive mind, I can examine my assumptions and interpretations to discover what actually fits the situation and what does not."

- "When people strongly and passionately assert their opinions and advocate their truth, making anyone who disagrees with them, including me, wrong, I will listen to them. I will hear their ardent advocacy as an opportunity to deepen my understanding of their point of view rather than getting hooked by hearing it as a challenge to my own views or to what's right."

- "I will advocate my point of view by owning it as mine only and offer it not as the truth, but as another valid perspective that also deserves to be understood."

As she pulled into the parking lot she saw more people than she expected pouring into the meeting hall. Some of them appeared to have brought signs to wave. With her stomach in knots she entered through the side door, walked to the front of the room and began to get situated. The room was arranged as she had requested. There was no podium, only a chair, side table for a glass of water, and a microphone. Seating was arranged in a horseshoe so people could see each other more easily. As she took off her coat, filled her water glass, and gazed around the room, she began to feel more relaxed. She took a moment to write down the key aspects of the Understanding Process she had gone over during her drive to the meeting and put them on the table next to her. As the starting time of the meeting approached, Maria found that part of herself was actually looking forward to this dialogue.

With little fanfare the meeting was convened by the coordinator of the satellite office. After welcoming those present, she turned the meeting over to Maria and took her seat. An awkward moment of silence was broken by Maria thanking the group for having her and telling them why she was there.

The gathering lasted about two hours. When it was over Maria and many of those who attended agreed that they had taken significant steps towards improving relations between the main and satellite offices. Most importantly they had made inroads into shifting their mind-models about each other. Whereas before the meeting both Maria and the staff had been interpreting each other's behavior as being dishonest and adversarial, now there was more willingness to entertain positive and hopeful interpretations. How did this shift occur? What supported it? Without getting into all the details of the meeting, an example will help us to see how Maria's use of the Understanding Process contributed to the outcome.

A particularly touchy issue was the library. The agency provided a well-stocked children's library for the purpose of encouraging parents to read to their children. The goal of this program was twofold: 1) to encourage parents to spend special time with their children, and 2) to improve reading ability and scores. As it turned out however, the library was hardly ever used and over time it evolved into a kind of catch-all storage space. Before this meeting Maria thought (like the board of directors and the agency director before her) that the staff and community were lazy, dumb, didn't care about education, didn't care about good parenting, and misused and wasted agency property. Of course this state of affairs raised the board's hackles every time this satellite office asked for more money and resources. "Why give them more when they don't appreciate or know how to use what they already have?" So when Maria asked to hear what was on people's minds, resources in general and the library in particular were at the top of the list.

Accusations from the staff and community flew fast and furiously. "You're cheap. Everyone else (the other satellite offices) gets the money they ask for except us. You don't give a damn about us, we could die out here and you wouldn't even know the difference. I'm sick and tired of your thinking you know what is best for us. We don't need a library just because you think we do." Reminding herself that this was an opportunity to understand perceptions and experiences clearly different from her own, Maria quelled the defensiveness she felt rising in her, and said, "Whoa...let's slow down. Clearly there is something very important here. But I'm afraid I'm not understanding what it is. Can you help me out?" The interchange continued:

"What else is there to say? Besides no one listens anyway. Why should we waste our breath?"

"It sounds like you haven't been listened to before. You're saying what you want and the main office doesn't pay attention."

"Yeah, something like that."

"I'm sorry that happened. It should not have. Someone mentioned the library, can we start there? Can someone help me to understand what the issue is?"

"We don't need a library, that's it."

"I'm wondering about something. What message did you get from the main office when that library was installed? What were they saying to you, so to speak? "

"I felt like I was being told that I don't know what is best for me and my children. I think they were trying to humiliate us with this library, to show how smart they are and how dumb we are."

"Did anyone else feel this way?"

"Yes."

"Please tell me more. I'm really missing something here. How does this library show you that you are dumb?"

"Look we do our best for our kids. But we didn't spend half of our lives in school like you did. We had to work, we still do."

"I know that. People in this community work very hard, and you care about your children. I apologize if I sound like a broken record, but I would really like to understand about the library. I still don't get how it makes you think we, the agency and the board, think you're dumb." Trying to stay connected to her curiosity and recognize her assumptions and interpretations as just that, not facts, Maria was struggling to keep her judgmentalism out of the way. The more people talked the more they fulfilled her worst stereotypes of them.

"Okay. I'll tell you. This is hard. But it's the truth. Many of the people that use the services of this agency can't read. They feel humiliated when they are just expected to be able to read to their children and they can't do it. For many of them their children read better than they do. How can we tell you, all of you main office people, that people here can't read when in your town even the taxi drivers have a college education. You take so much for granted."

Maria was stunned. She had imagined many explanations for the library problem, but never this. The staff and community people were talking about an experience, functional illiteracy, that she knew absolutely nothing about.

"I'm so sorry that we humiliated you. I can assure you that it was not on purpose. If we had paid attention to what you were saying, if we had really listened, this would never have happened, at least I hope it would not have happened. And I'll be perfectly honest with you. I don't know anything about what it is like not to be able to read. Please help me to understand what that experience is like."

After listening and absorbing quietly and respectfully for over an hour as people spoke about their experiences, Maria took the risk to ask, "I wonder what we at the main office must have looked like to you, what it must have been like for you to work with us. Given all that you have shared, I can't imagine it was positive." It wasn't. People told Maria in no uncertain terms how she and the rest of the management team were perceived. Occasionally the serious atmosphere was pierced by gales of laughter, including Maria's, as people painted verbal caricatures and did impersonations of their perceptions of Maria and the board of directors.

Toward the end of the meeting everyone who wanted to had shared their views on a number of issues, and Maria confirmed that she understood what they has said. She then offered to the group alternative perspectives to those that had been shared so far, some of which, Maria told them, were her own. She emphasized that neither she nor they held the whole truth about the situation and she did not want or expect them to agree with all she had to say. Inviting people to consider how everyone from within their own point of view was right, how everyone held a very important piece to a large and complex puzzle, Maria validated everyone's experience and truth. The agency was headed in a new and more promising direction.

Conclusion

One of the most heartening outcomes in these examples, especially the second one, was the transformation from cynicism to hope for and belief in the future. If "a cynic is not merely one who reads bitter lessons from the past; he (or she) is one who is prematurely disappointed in the future,"[33] it appears as if we are suffering a population explosion of cynics. Considering that cynicism, the step-child of the Debate Culture, flows rampant through so many of our public (and private) conversations, bruising our spirits and corroding our dreams even before they have a chance to take shape, this framework for dialogue holds promise.

Key Learning Points Reviewed

With the Understanding Process in hand, Maria's courage
to address the concerns of a group of people with long-standing
complaints about the agency and suspicions about her was
clearly heightened. She also built up her confidence by heeding
the written reminders she provided to herself. As a result
Maria's approach to the potentially incendiary situation
was nearly fail safe.
Operating out of the mind-set of the Understanding Process
(as well as engaging in the behaviors germane to it) she was
able to transform a volatile situation into an informative and
productive conversation. Maria's efforts to truly understand the
complaints of the participants from within their frame-of-reference established an atmosphere of goodwill. As the evening
progressed, blaming and judging gave way to collaboration
and hope for the future.

PART III

GOING FORWARD

10

Frequently Asked Questions

*Curiosity is one of the most permanent and
certain characteristics of a vigorous intellect.*
Samuel Johnson

1. **The Understanding Process is easy for me to do. Is it
supposed to be difficult?**

   Generally people find it easy when they agree with or don't
   have strong feelings about what is being said. It is more
   challenging when we don't agree, when something important
   seems to be at stake, when we feel threatened or when there is
   conflict about values.

2. **As a salesperson I think I'm already practicing
The Understanding Process. What is the difference
between the sales process and The Understanding Process?**

   The key difference is in the intention you bring. In sales the
   goal is to sell something to someone. The main purpose of the
   Understanding Process is to understand a person from their
   point of view and to enter into dialogue. Dialogue is "outcome
   free" in the sense that, when we begin, we don't know what will

happen in the interaction, or where it will lead. As Buber points out, "Genuine dialogue cannot be arranged before-hand."[34] Nonetheless understanding a customer's point of view and needs could certainly benefit the sales process. Customer satisfaction would probably increase and along with it loyalty.

3. **Isn't it possible that someone could understand where a person is coming from and use it against them?**

   Yes. Behaviors, disguised as a search for understanding, can be used to accomplish goals such as, winning, selling or persuading. The key question is, "What is your intention or goal?" If it is to win or to be right, you are in the Conventional Discussion Process mode even though you are using Understanding Process behaviors. Don't confuse Understanding Process behaviors with the process itself. This process is fundamentally about intention. Whether you use Understanding Process behaviors in the service of the Conventional Discussion Process or not is an ethical choice. It's up to you.

4. **When I used the Understanding Process it was hard to find anything to say because I agreed with what my partner was saying. Am I missing something?**

   Remember you may be agreeing for different reasons. Not understanding why people hold the perspectives that they do can result in erroneously believing that we are in agreement with someone, when in fact we are not. Because we have never truly explored an issue with someone, we may leap to the false conclusion that "they think like me."

5. **Doesn't the Understanding Process amount to colluding with people who are prejudiced and narrow-minded? Doesn't understanding them just encourage them?**

   Using the Understanding Process with a person whose behavior or opinions you disagree with or find abhorrent, and not letting them know that you disagree or disapprove, may leave you feeling that you are colluding with them. However there is nothing precluding you from expressing your perspective. It is perfectly acceptable to advocate your point of view by letting the other person know early in the conversation that you hold another opinion, and that you do not agree with what you have heard them say or with what they did. Nonetheless you can tell them that you are still interested in understanding their perspective, what it means for them, and how they came to have it. Or after you have listened to and understood what they are saying, tell them your perspective. Generally after being listened to deeply and truly understood, people are willing to be more generous and gracious in listening to views different from their own.

6. **When should we not use the Understanding Process?**

We don't want to replace the Conventional Discussion Process hammer with an Understanding Process hammer. This process does not work in every situation. Ask yourself, "What does this situation call for?" Immediate decision and action? Is harm being done to someone or some thing and must be stopped? Am I in the proper frame of mind to bring the Understanding Process intention to this situation? Or first, do I need time to reflect? Do I need to cool off? Would it be helpful for me to talk with someone not involved in the situation, someone who, as they listened to me, would help sort out my thoughts and feelings?

7. **Since the Understanding Process isn't about staking out a position and defending it, won't it leave me feeling vulnerable to being attacked by someone who is using the Conventional Discussion Process?**

No not necessarily. Generally when people use the Understanding Process with someone who is in the Conventional Discussion mode, the tone of the entire interaction changes. In response to being listened to and understood, the person using the Conventional Discussion Process tends to become calmer, less defensive and more relaxed. Because they are being listened to rather than challenged or attacked, they don't have to behave defensively by challenging or attacking you.

Typically the more we assert ourselves by assuming the frame of mind and using the behaviors of the Conventional Discussion Process, the more vulnerable we think we will be if we shift to the Understanding Process. However once we make the shift we discover that, as a client noted, "I didn't feel vulnerable, like I thought I would, because there was no attack from the other person after I began to truly listen to them."

8. **If the interaction doesn't go into a debate, it doesn't feel like I've done anything.**

This raises a deeper question, "What does 'doing something' mean"? If "doing something" means persuading, selling or winning, then one could very well feel as if nothing was accomplished by using the Understanding Process. On the other hand if learning and developing insight by listening and understanding counts as doing something then using the Understanding Process is a means to a valuable end.

In any given situation it is useful to ask, "In this situation, what would count as doing something effective and of value?" There are times when what is called for is strongly expressing your opinion about a matter, when you want to convince others of your point of view. In those instances Conventional Discussion Process behaviors are more appropriate to the matter at hand.

9. **Isn't the Understanding Process the same as conflict resolution or management?**

No. Although the Understanding Process can be used effectively as part of a conflict resolution process, in and of itself, it is not about resolving conflicts. Rather than a vehicle for resolving differences, the Understanding Process is intended to:

1) help us to discover our differences (and similarities),
2) deeply understand the nature of our differences and why we
agree and disagree, and 3) improve how people with strong
differences regard and relate to each other.

10. **What's the point of using the Understanding Process if it has
no particular outcome other than to understand others from
their point of view? What about *action*?**

It is true that the intended outcome of the Understanding
Process is not task-oriented. Nonetheless the Understanding
Process, especially because it involves listening deeply to
people, is very valuable in determining what action is truly
useful in any given situation. Listening unconditionally allows
us to hear what needs to be done in that moment and in
the future. Listening also helps us to hear when it is better not
to act. How many times have actions been taken at any level
(interpersonal, organizational or international) with the
best of intentions and less than desirable results occur
because we have not truly understood what was needed?

11. **What if someone is deceptive and I don't trust them to be
honest with me when using the Understanding Process? I'm
concerned that I will believe them and later be unpleasantly
surprised.**

First of all, trust your own good sense about people. If you
feel that someone is being dishonest with you, hold your
perception as a hypothesis, a possibility. If and when you have
enough information to confirm it you will need to decide if
you think it is better to confront the situation or to just be
careful about what you believe and what you divulge. In any
event people are just as they are, despite our protests to the
contrary.
   Regarding the Understanding Process, it may nonetheless be
helpful for you to try to understand that person from within
their mind-models of the world. The goal is not to change
them. You can't anyway. However by understanding them on

their terms you might gain insight into how to handle the situation.

12. **When I am accustomed to someone responding to me with debate and argument and they suddenly change to listening and trying to understand me, I feel put off and I'm wondering, "What are they up to?"**

It can be disconcerting when people change familiar behaviors, even when it's a change for the better. In this situation you can use the Understanding Process to inquire about the change in behavior that you notice. For instance you can make an observation about the difference and then ask your friend or colleague to help you to understand it. As for the situation the other person is in, it is often helpful to quell possible distrust by acknowledging that you are interacting differently than you usually do, perhaps because your usual style of being the devil's advocate isn't as rewarding anymore.

13. **Considering the prevalence of the Debate Culture, are there public examples where the Understanding Process is used on a regular basis? Where can I look?**

Pay attention to some interviewers. Sometimes, regardless of who is being interviewed, whether it's a beloved public figure or a murderer on death row, the interviewer approaches the person with a desire to understand them rather than to impose their (the interviewer's) own perspective. A few television news moderators pose Understanding Process inquiries to their guests who hold divergent opinions rather than set up an argument between the parties. Another suggestion is to just listen to people talk to each other. Occasionally you will notice people are actually listening, inquiring, and truly trying to understand one another.

14. **I like the Understanding Process, but it takes so long. Realistically we don't have time for it, do we?**

Before answering this question in more depth I want to draw our attention to an assumption implied within it. Namely conventional discussion takes less time than the Understanding Process.

Many of us probably experience conventional discussion as being faster than dialogue for a couple of reasons. Because we are more familiar with it, conventional discussion seems to come naturally to us. We can probably do it in our sleep. It seems fast and efficient. When we begin to practice interacting with others using the Understanding Process we encounter a learning curve. We stumble and fall as we seek to understand others, especially those with whom we strongly disagree, the ones who "push our buttons." As we become more adept at dialogue, both as a way of thinking and interact-ing, our facility with it will make it go faster.

Another reason conventional discussion appears to be faster is that it has the tendency to silence the "losing side." The conversation comes to a screeching halt, silence is interpreted as agreement, and "time is saved." Because multiple views are not explored for the value they have to offer, we do finish on time, if not early. The question is, "Have we really saved time or are we merely going fast now only to get derailed later?"

Recall a situation in which you lost a debate or an argument and felt silenced into pseudo-agreement. (I assume we all have experienced this at some time or another.) Despite how the decision was made, you are expected to "get with the program" and support the winning position. After all, your silence means that you concede "being right" to the other side. What happens next? At best we don't do anything. We just stand by. We don't obstruct progress, but we don't do any thing to support it either. At worst we do all we can to undermine its success. The more forces we can muster in opposition to the "winner" the better.

Is using the Conventional Discussion Process in this way really faster than understanding and dialogue? Or are we forever becoming stuck and starting over? Are we getting anywhere at all, except burned-out? Although using the Understanding Process to explore different points of view may take more time initially, in the end it may actually save time. As another trainer once said, "We go slow now in order to go fast later."

Finally remember that the Understanding Process not only describes a way of behaving as we interact with others, it is a way of thinking and listening as well. This being the case we can shift our attention to being curious about and open to what is being said. We can focus our listening on "What's new? Of value? What can I learn?" Shifting our internal process from conventional discussion mode to that of understanding means listening from a vantage point different from that to which most of us have been socialized in our Debate Culture. Listening in this way does not necessarily take more time. It does, however, take practice.

11

Conclusion

---

*The difference between misery and happiness
depends on what we do with our attention.*
                                    Sharon Salzberg

We have a choice in how we interact with each other. We need not succumb to the pull of the Debate Culture. Essentially we have been exploring *how* the manner in which we talk with each other strongly influences the kinds of relationships, organizations, worlds, and cultures we create. In the face of deadlocks and stalemates, stuck relationships, and static organizations, we have discovered that we can do something different that will make a difference for the better.

In comparing two modes of interaction, the Conventional Discussion Process and the Understanding Process, we discovered that the former tends to be pervasive, the dominant mode of conversing in a wide range of contexts, while the latter is less widely embraced. As a result we unwittingly generate adversarial debates and miss opportunities to embrace the richness of our differences with interest and wonder rather than defensiveness and fear. When faced with these predicaments, or merely in the interest of generating insight, pursuing new connections, and building flexible, responsive relationships and organizations, we have learned that we can choose something other than conventional discussion and by so doing create new and different outcomes. We can enter into dialogue through practicing the Understanding Process, and possibly, when opportunities arise and if we choose, foster the growth of a Dialogue Culture.

The origins of the Understanding Process are rooted in an ongoing quest to find outcomes different from those typically generated by our habitual tendency to lapse into debate and argument. Used unconsciously and repeatedly, we learned that conventional discussion is a means by which we create separations, "mine vs. yours" and "us vs. them", which require defending. The more we identify with our position, the stronger we defend it and the more threatened we feel by different points of view. The very act of defending, often best accomplished by subtlety or overtly attacking, further sharpens the demarcations which require ever stronger modes of defense. This process of separation fosters objectification through stereotyping and negative labeling, which in turn fuels even greater distancing and objectification. Judgments and criticisms, spoken as well as unspoken, infect our interactions. It's a self-reinforcing, spiraling process that takes on a life of its own leaving often unintended consequences in its wake. Chronic debate is destructive, and despite our best intentions, it takes us down a path that leads in the opposite direction from where we say we want to go. Joan Tollifson eloquently reminds us about the nature of this all too familiar experience:

(When) I feel completely identified with my position the existence of an opposing or different position provokes fear, anger, feelings of separation and all the pain of that. I know I am right. It feels horrible.

I become so ridiculously opinionated that I cannot stop myself from speaking up. I watch how attached I am to my opinions and their importance, how irritated and threatened I feel by those whose views are different...I am instantly convinced that what I'm accustomed to is better...The judgments come so quickly, the labels I slap onto other people... unfamiliar ways of behaving.

How easily we humans polarize things, creating enemies in the name of a new and better world.[35]

We can hear in Tollifson's words an invitation to be aware of how we can be so habituated to conventional discussion that we don't even know that we are doing it and how difficult it is to stop. In all contexts, without thinking about it, we slide into a kind of talk that pits us and our ideas against each other. As a result even the most commonplace encounters can be subtlety infused with tension and discord that, although difficult to pin-point, are nonetheless unwelcome and disconcerting.

It's important to recall that debate, or "putting something on trial to see if it is wanting or not,"[36] in and of itself, is not inherently a problem. Our unthinking, habitual use of it, which is encouraged by our Debate Culture, is. This is when debate becomes destructive. No longer just a tool capable of reaping rewards when applied appropriately, it generates fear and defensiveness, with the inevitable consequences of creating separations and staking out positions that need to be protected. Such circumstances make it difficult if not impossible for us to embrace critical differences among ourselves and simply converse honestly and respectfully about the things that matter most to us, especially when they are challenged by others.

It is to this wanting state of affairs that alternatives are needed, antidotes that are accessible and can produce real benefits when put into practice. By noticing what happens when (especially in the face of real or perceived differences in beliefs and values) people connect rather than separate, continue treating each other respectfully and humanely rather than objectifying one another, that a picture of the possible begins to emerge. Familiar themes such as listening, understanding, not being quick to judge, and walking in another's shoes repeatedly surface, reminding us why they hold the positions of honor they do in a multitude of ancient wisdom traditions as well as in respected contemporary approaches to successful and rewarding human interaction and organization. These themes, among others, are the strands that have been woven together to create the Understanding Process.

Hopefully, you will continue to practice and explore this approach to dialogue.

Putting Theory Into Practice

One consequence of the persuasiveness of the Debate Culture is our tendency to equate intelligence with being able to argue well. To brilliantly assert and defend our own position and critically dismantle the opposition is generally valued and rewarded. In such a climate being smart and clever is equated with being critical, picking holes in whatever the other person is saying. This is not a question of whether we necessarily like to find flaws and faults or not, it's a matter of what our collective consensus mind model has determined "smart" to mean.

What are the implications of this for practicing the Understanding Process? After all if being intelligent, thoughtful and "holding your own" requires crafting your rebuttal instead of truly listening, then is it possible to practice the Understanding Process and still be "smart"? The answer is a resounding, Yes! It simply requires that you think differently about how you "do" conversation. You can stand on your own without resorting to conventional discussion. In fact by listening quietly, deeply and with a sense of curiosity and interest, you will likely discover another kind of intelligence. Subtle perceptions and provocative, generative insights to ponder and inquire about, normally obscured by the tunnel vision required for "scoring points," will emerge into view. By letting go of the need to know your destination (making points, winning, persuading) ahead of time, you open yourself to generating new discoveries through dialogue with others.

Practicing the Understanding Process can be uncomfortable at first. The more accustomed we are to interacting in the Conventional Discussion mode, the better socialized we are in Debate Culture, the more awkward it is to try something else. It can be especially challenging to work through the feeling (and belief) that we necessarily are "safer" using conventional discussion than dialogue, especially in situations in which we feel threatened. It is the process of conventional discussion itself that often creates the fractured situation that leaves us feeling defensive. In spite of this we once again turn to debate with the hope that "this time we will win" and safely prevail.

Indeed embracing the Understanding Process in such circumstances does, at least initially, call for a leap of faith. However it gets easier the more we practice. As with anything new there is a learning curve. Stay with it. Play with it. Have fun with it. Initially engage in dialogue in situations that are not highly emotionally charged for you. Then gradually move on to increasingly difficult circumstances, for example, those which you would have avoided in the past, not because it was the wisest thing to do but because you didn't have an alternative. As you continue to practice you will notice a gradual shift in your perspective. Difficult and complex situations will less often be perceived as quagmires best to be avoided and instead, increasingly be seen as approachable opportunities. Curiosity, concern and interest, supported by humble self-confidence and skillfulness gradually come to outweigh knee-jerk fearfulness and trepidation.

When setting out to build your competency it is helpful to focus on one aspect of the Understanding Process at a time, bringing it to the foreground of your attention. For example, you could:

- Practice eliciting multiple points of view on a matter with your conversation partners. Deliberately consider perspectives that are not held by those with whom you happen to be conversing. You can ask, "What do you think this situation looks like from so-and-so's standpoint?" Or "What if we didn't assume 'that' (whatever it is) and assumed 'this' instead. Then how would we perceive this situation?"

- Stay focused on the goal, understanding what's going on for someone else from within their point of view, their mind models. Keep reminding yourself about your intention to do this. When you "fall off your intention" (we all do at times), without self-incrimination, just "get back on."

- Practice suspending judgment. To do this, become aware of your internal process. Notice when you make a judgment or criticism. Just notice and resist acting on it. Don't beat your self up. Just be aware of it and put the judgment on the back burner. Shift your attention to connecting with the part of you that is more curious than judgmental. Listen from that place. Also use the Understanding Process with yourself. Help yourself to understand what your judgment and criticism is about. What are the feelings and assumptions behind it? Clarify your thoughts by writing in a journal.

• Listen, just listen. When you feel the urge to "jump in," stay put and pay attention to what is being said. If you feel yourself reacting, interpret it as a signal to practice reflection instead. You can take note of your internal reaction without its automatically being a trigger for action. Experience what it feels like to note it, non-judgmentally, and to let it pass rather than feeding it more energy by acting on it. Notice the impact of this on your interaction with the other person(s).

• Find occasions to work with listening to strong opinions as an opportunity to deepen your understanding of perspectives different from your own. One way to do this is to deliberately engage with ideas and listen to people with whom you usually disagree. Talk radio and television can be good sources.

• Bring assumptions to light, your own and others, for the purpose of deepening understanding rather than dethroning what someone else is saying. To unearth assumptions notice when you and others "predict" what will happen. An assumption is hidden in the prediction. Or pay attention to what you think you and others believe someone should, must, or never do or say. Therein lie assumptions, the foundation stones of our mind models.

• Work with advocating your thoughts and opinions by saying things like, "Here's another way to look at this," rather than "No it's like this."

Remember the more you work with the Understanding Process in a variety of different contexts the more it will bear fruit for you. The seven key learnings explored in Chapter 3 are just a sampling of what's possible. The common thread among them is that it takes time for your practice to bring rewards.

Recall that you can change the course of an interaction by shifting to the Understanding Process. You don't need to get an agreement ahead of time from the other person. Also in order for it to be beneficial, it isn't necessary to start a crusade to get everyone to use it.

This raises another point. In settings in which the Understanding Process has been introduced to a group, it is counterproductive to use it as a standard against which to measure other people and whether they are engaging in dialogue or not. If and when you feel the impulse to point out someone else's failure it is a clear indication that you yourself are not functioning from within it. Ask yourself, "What could I understand better and what can I do to help myself to improve my understanding?"

Recognizing your true intention is critical if you want to reap the benefits of being in dialogue. Sometimes we want to seek to understand but our judgments seem to get the best of us; they leak through our most valiant efforts to stay in dialogue. We can also engage in Understanding Process behaviors, but our real intention is to win the argument. Setting someone up to knock them down is a device common to debate and argument. Both of these situations contaminate the well of trust and relationship building and undercut the other benefits of engaging in dialogue as distinct from debate.

The former situation is familiar to anyone who practices with dialogue and there are ways to work with it. Most importantly be honest with yourself. If you are reacting with strong judgments and are unable to work with them in the ways suggested above, try the following. Simply say something like, "I want to tell you what's going on with me as I listen to you so that we can keep the lines of communication open. I'm trying to understand you and not be judgmental, but it's hard for me. I have different views. You probably know that. I'm concerned that my 'less than understanding' reactions are leaking out and that you might think I'm writing you off. I'm not. I'm struggling. I do want to understand your point of view. I hope you are willing to continue talking with me."

When sharing the Understanding Process, as well as the Conventional Discussion Process, keep mind-models in mind. Just as my mind-models influenced the development of these two processes, so yours will influence your interpretations of them (likewise for those with whom you share these methods). There are both drawbacks and advantages to be gained from this inevitability.

First, the drawbacks. Mind-models both filter information out of and into our awareness. As discussed earlier that which is unfamiliar and does not fit within an already existing aspect of our mind-models gets filtered out. Data that is similar in some way to something that already exists in our mind-models registers in our awareness. When we are introduced to something new, like the Understanding Process, we quickly identify those aspects of it that are similar to things that we already know. This is fine, as far as it goes. It helps us to learn. "Oh. This (new) is like that (familiar). I know about that, therefore, I know this."

As we work to grasp new information we have a tendency to equate it to that which is already known to us. For example, it is not uncommon for people just introduced to the Understanding Process to observe, "This is conflict management," or "This is just like what we do in sales, try to understand the customer's needs." The trouble is that those aspects of the Understanding Process that are truly new get lost because they have no place to adhere to within their mind-models. This process is not just another name for conflict management or effective sales, even though it can be beneficial to both.

This presents a challenge. How can we prevent those unfamiliar parts from getting lost? How can we help people to stay open to discovering something new? One thing we can do is remind people about mind-models and that they are likely filtering out that for which they don't yet have an internal model. Invite them to stay open to the idea that they don't necessarily fully "get it". Additionally we can encourage people to talk about their experiences with and interpretation of understanding and dialogue. By listening carefully and seeking to understand them, and, as we develop more insight into the process ourselves, we will be able to help people to create frames-of-reference they can use to anchor their new experiences and insights.

This brings me to the benefits. Precisely because all of us necessarily interpret and experience the Understanding Process through our own mind-models, new insights into it are limitless. Exploring those insights with each other is another way to mine its potential richness. I never cease to gain deeper insight into the value of the process from colleagues and clients who inevitably bring their own perspectives to it.

Finally, now that you have begun to practice and reap the benefits of the Understanding Process, the extent to which conventional discussion patterns habitually enter into conversations will probably begin to jump out at you. Pay attention to your reactions to this. Do you find that, because you now know of another way to interact, you increasingly notice missed opportunities to gain deeper understanding and discover new meanings and perspectives? Pay attention to the nature of the conversations around you. Listen to people conversing on the bus, at a restaurant at the table next to you, on a radio or TV talk show. Notice what people, especially those socialized in the Western tradition, say and do.

Recently I was eating lunch at a "community table" in a local restaurant. Two middle-aged women friends sat down at the same table. After a few bites of lunch and mutual congratulations on how healthfully they were eating, they launched into a discussion about religion and the right of a religious group to impose its beliefs on others. The first woman set the stage by describing a fictional pre-industrial hunting and gathering society untouched by modern society except for the anthropologists that had spent time with them. She asked her lunch partner, "So you think it's okay for people of your faith to intrude into their lives, now that they have been 'discovered', and convert these people to your faith even though they are perfectly happy believing just as they do?"

"Yes, of course," was the unequivocal, matter-of-fact reply.

"You have no right to do this. You are stripping them of their culture. You are assuming your religion is superior to theirs. That's sheer arrogance!"

"No they just think they are happy with their beliefs, they don't know any better. They don't know how much happier they could be. It's my obligation, or that of the missionaries of my faith, to impart this to them. It's a gift. Your, 'live and let live' philosophy only leads to immorality, or amorality at best. That's what's wrong with the world today, you know."

And so it went. Perhaps they were having a good time debating, but I think not. Their body language changed from leaning close to each other to sitting farther apart. By the end of their conversation they had turned the trunks of their bodies away from each other and folded their arms across their chests.

Maybe they didn't know how else to talk about this topic that clearly engaged both of them. But as I was unabashedly eavesdropping I heard so many things to which the other could have responded, "Help me to understand..." I wondered if they were curious about why the other held the strong views that she did. From my vantage point it seemed like there were rich opportunities to truly listen to and learn from and about each other, to deepen understanding about perspectives radically different from their own and in the process gain more insight into their own point of view. Also, on the face of it, this appeared to be one of those situations in which agreement was immaterial and in which "winning" would surely leave open the question about what was actually won.

As I reflected on my own perspective on their topic I realized that even though I too am of the opinion that it is unacceptable to try to convert people I was curious as to how the woman, who apparently believed similarly, had come to her view. And why was she defending it so energetically? Since I consider this a moral point of view, I found myself curious about how this perspective was perceived as immoral by the other woman. What assumptions were we making about what is moral or not? What is the nature of the mind-models specific to these two people and myself that support and reinforce these different points of view? How did our own mind-models influence how we interpreted each other's words and behaviors? Layers upon layers of rich possibilities to explore unfolded in my reverie. From within this mental framework, winning and losing, asserting positions and challenging others seemed uninteresting and fruitless compared to what the Understanding Process could reap.

We are continuously presented with opportunities to consciously choose the manner in which we will relate. We need not unthinkingly conform to the expectations of the Debate Culture. We can intentionally resist the urge, however subtle, to be right or maintain the appearance of being right, by making others wrong in some way. We can stem our habitual tendencies for conventional discussion modes of interaction. Instead we can opt to discover the rewards of practicing the Understanding Process to transform our conversations. The opportunities to explore the applications and benefits of entering into dialogue are limitless.

ENDNOTES

1. J.I. Rodale, *The Synonym Finder (Warner Books Edition)* (New York: Warner Books, 1986), p. 303.

2. Chris Argyris and Donald Schon, *Theory in Practice* (San Francisco: Jossey-Bass, 1974); Mary Field Belenky, et al; *Women's Ways of Knowing* (New York: Basic Books, 1986); David Bohm, *On Dialogue* (Ojai, CA: David Bohm Seminars, 1990); Martin Buber, *I and Thou* (New York: Charles Scribner's Sons, 1958); Martin Buber, *The Knowledge of Man* (London: George Allen & Unwin Ltd, 1965); Ram Dass and Mirabai Bush, *Compassion In Action* (New York: Bell Tower, 1992); Peter Elbow, *Writing Without Teachers* (London: Oxford University Press, 1973); Maurice Freidman, *Martin Buber: The Life of Dialogue* (Chicago: University of Chicago Press, 1960); Joseph Goldstein, *Insight Meditation* (Boston: Shambala, 1994); Joseph Goldstein and Jack Kornfield, *Seeking the Heart of Wisdom* (Boston: Shambala, 1987); William Issacs, "Dialogue," in *The Fifth Discipline Fieldbook*, ed. Peter Senge et al. (New York: Currency Doubleday, 1994); Sharon Salzberg, *Loving-Kindness* (Boston: Shambala, 1995); The Dalai Lama, *The Power of Compassion* (San Francisco: Thorsons, 1995); The Dalai Lama, *The Good Heart* (Boston: Wisdom Publications, 1996); The Dialogue Group, *Reflections on Building Blocks and Guidelines* for Dialogue (Laguna Hills, CA: The Dialogue Group, 1988); Joan Tollifson, *Bare-Bones Meditation* (New York: Bell Tower, 1996).

3. Maurice Freidman, Martin Buber: *The Life of Dialogue* (Chicago: University of Chicago Press, 1960), p. 87.

4. I want to thank my friend and scholar, Mary Scheidler, for identifying "the dialogue between experience and theory."

5. Linda Chavez, "As In Israel, We Need To Tone Down Rhetoric," *USA Today*, 8 Nov. 1995, Sec. A, p. 15.

6. William Raspberry, "We would all be better off if...," *Boulder Daily Camera*, 27 Aug. 1997, Sec. A, p. 10.

7. Hillary Rodham Clinton, "Rabin's Murder Was Attack on Democracy," *Boulder Daily Camera*, 12 Nov. 1995, Sec. F, p. 3.

8. Cornel West and Michael Lerner, "After O.J. and the Farrakhan-led Million Man March: Is Healing Possible?" *Tikkun*, Vol. 10, No. 6, p. 18.

9. Melissa Healy, "New Movement Plots More Civil Way of Living," *Los Angeles Times*, Home Edition, 12 Dec. 1996, Sec. A, p. 1; Jill Lawrence, "Excuse Me, But Whatever Happened To Manners? Wanted: Good Citizens," *USA Today*, 16 Dec. 1996, Sec. A, p. 1; Julia Malone, "Clinton to Challenge Americans to Return to Civility, Responsibility," *The Atlanta Journal & Constitution*, 7 Jun. 1995, Sec. A, p. 7; Mimi Hall, "White House Names Advisory Board on Race," *USA Today*, 13 Jun. 1997; Ronald Brownstein, "Clinton Seeks Dialogue on Race, But He Must Go Beyond the Same Old Talk," *Los Angeles Times*, Home Edition, 12 Jul. 1997; Jane Gross, "'Day of Dialogue' Tries to Span Racial Gulf," *Los Angeles Times*, 25 Oct. 1995, Sec. A, p. 1; Richard Chasin et al., "From Diatribe to Dialogue on Divisive Public Issues: Approaches Drawn from Family Therapy," in *Mediation Quarterly*, Summer, 1996, p. 323; Glenda Valentine, "Inquire Within: Workshops Help Teachers Talk About Prejudice and Discrimination," in *Teaching Tolerance*, Fall, 1996, p. 60; David Ruenzel, "Crucial Conversations: Study Circles Help Students Talk Constructively about Race," in *Teaching Tolerance*, Spring, 1997, p. 19; "Beyond Right or Wrong: A Conversation Between Pema Chodron and bell hooks," in *The Sun*, June 1997, p. 11; Jim Martin, "Dialogue Can Replace Incivility, Impatience," *Boulder Daily Camera*, 16 Jun. 1997, op-ed page; Annie Hill, "Workshop Seeks Civil Dialogue: US Public Discourse Seen As Bitter, Divisive," *Boulder Daily Camera*, 15 Jun. 1997, Sec. B, p. 1.

10. Peter Elbow, *Writing Without Teachers* (London: Oxford University Press, 1973), p. 173.

11. Victor Frankel addresses this at length in *The Doctor and the Soul*, 2nd. ed. (New York: Vintage Books, 1986).

12. Peter Elbow, *Writing Without Teachers* (London: Oxford University Press, 1973), p. 177.

13. Ram Dass and Mirabai Bush, *Compassion In Action* (New York: Bell Tower, 1992), p. 169.

14. Joan Tollifson, *Bare-Bones Meditation* (New York: Bell Tower, 1996), p. 135.

15. Martin Buber, *The Knowledge of Man* (London: George Allen & Unwin Ltd, 1965), p. 85-86.

16. Martin Buber, *The Knowledge of Man* (London: George Allen & Unwin Ltd, 1965), p. 87-88.

17. I want to thank my friend and colleague, Keith Langeneckert, for suggesting the addition of the "truth sayer."

18. Maurice Freidman, Martin Buber: *The Life of Dialogue* (Chicago: University of Chicago Press, 1960), p. 88.

19. The Dalai Lama, *The Good Heart* (Boston: Wisdom Publications,1996), p. 15.

20. The Dalai Lama, *The Good Heart* (Boston: Wisdom Publications, 1996), p. 15.

21. The Dalai Lama, *The Good Heart* (Boston: Wisdom Publications, 1996), p. 15.

22. "Leading a Diverse Workforce," US West pluralism workshop.

23. Sandra L. Bem, "Gender Schema Theory and Its Implications for Child Development: Raising Gender Aschematic Children in a Gender Schematic Society," in Signs: Journal of Women in Culture and Society, Volume 8, 1983, p. 598-616.

24. Peter M. Senge, et al., *The Fifth Discipline Fieldbook* (New York: Doubleday, 1994), p. 235-293.

25. Margaret Wheatley and Myron Kellner-Rogers, *A Simpler Way* (San Francisco: Berret-Kholer Publishers, 1996), p. 49.

26. Margaret Wheatley and Myron Kellner-Rogers, *A Simpler Way* (San Francisco: Berret-Kholer Publishers, 1996), p. 49.

27. I want to thank my colleague, Phyllis Henderson, for introducing me to the concept of the beach ball.

28. My friend and colleague, Pamela Bliss, extended the beach ball metaphor with the idea of "painting" the beachball and graciously suggested including it.

29. Peggy MacIntosh, "White Privilege and Male Privilege: A Personal Account of Coming to See Correspondences Through Work In Women Studies" (Wellesley, MA: College Center for Research on Women, 1988).

30. Lewis Carroll, *Alice in Wonderland and Through the Looking Glass* (New York: Grosset & Dunlap Publishers), p. 229-230.

31. Elaine McShulskis, "HRM Update: Help New Managers Succeed," in HRM Magazine, January, 1998, p. 21-22 (appears in ch. 8).

32. I want to thank Glenna Gerard for introducing me to the importance of review and reflection as a means of deepening learning and insight.

33. Robert Andrews, *The Columbia Dictionary of Quotations* (New York: Columbia University Press, 1993), p. 210.

34. Martin Buber, *The Knowledge of Man* (London: George Allen & Unwin Ltd., 1965), p. 87.

35. Joan Tollifson, *Bare-Bones Meditation* (New York: Bell Tower, 1996), p. 53 and 56.

36. Peter Elbow, *Writing Without Teachers* (London: Oxford University Press, 1973), p. 173.

About the Author

DR.DEBORAH L.FLICK is an internationally recognized expert in dialogue and diversity and the owner and founder of Collaborative Solutions Group, an international consulting firm specializing in communication, leadership, dialogue and diversity. With over 25 years of experience, Dr. Flick consults with and conducts training for Fortune 50 corporations, local and federal governments, international non-government organizations, medical and behavioral health facilities, private non-profits, colleges and universities, and unions.

During her fourteen-year tenure on the faculty of the University of Colorado, Boulder, she taught courses in dialogue, leadership, women in the workplace, workplace diversity, and the legal, economic, and social impact of sexual harassment.

Frequently invited to give presentations at conferences, Dr. Flick has presented to the National Multicultural Institute, the American Association of Higher Education, Lucent Technologies Global Diversity Conference, Annual Colorado EEO/AA Conference, National Gender Diversity Conference, and the Annual National Diversity Conference. In 1977 Dr. Flick founded and directed the non-profit organization, Denver Safehouse for Battered Women.

Dr. Flick earned her Ph.D. in Communication from the University of Colorado, Boulder and her MA in Psychology from Sonoma State University, Rhonert Park, CA. She received the "Teaching Excellence Award" from the University of Colorado and appears in *Who's Who in American Universities and Colleges* and *Who's Who of American Women*.

Dr. Flick is an invited guest expert on national radio broadcasts and has been featured in *Training* and *Business Week*. She is also a columnist for *Colorado Woman News*.

ORDER FORM

To order *From Debate to Dialogue: Using the Understanding Process to Transform Our Conversations* and related products, please complete this form and return to:

ORCHID
PUBLICATIONS

P.O. Box 895
Boulder, CO 80306-0895

Quantity discounts
are available for training
programs and other
company uses.

QUANTITY	PRODUCTS	PRICE	TOTAL
_____	From Debate to Dialogue: Using the Understanding Process To Transform Our Conversations	$14.95	$_____
_____	"Understanding Process and Conventional Discussion Chart" Colorful 8 1/2" x11" Laminated Chart	$ 3.00	$_____
	Colorado Residents add 4.15%		$_____
	Sub-Total		$_____

Shipping & Handling:

For Orders Totaling:	Add:	
Up to $30.00	$5.00	
$30.01 to $70	$7.00	
$70.01 to $100	$10.00	
Over $100	$13.00	$_____

TOTAL ENCLOSED $_____

Please make checks or money orders payable to Orchid Publications.

PLEASE SHIP ORDER TO:

Name_____

Company Name_____

Address_____

City_____State_____Zip_____

Phone (   )_____Email_____

For more information call (303) 443-5677 or e-mail drdflick@qwest.net

Thank you very much for your order.